NON
INDI

This easy-to-follow cookery book presents a wide range of non-vegetarian recipes to the common housewife as also the lover of the culinary art. There are a number of delicious preparations given under each chapter, e.g., Pulao or Biriani, Stuffed Parathas, Curries, Chops and Tikkas, and include the author's own specialities. The comprehensive contents and a detailed glossary add to the readability of the book.

Pritam Uberoi, who has dedicated herself to the culinary art for nearly four decades, needs no introduction to the many thousands of her pupils and admirers. She was Director, Delhi School of Cookery, and also taught at Lady Irwin College. Recognised as one of the best teachers of cookery Mrs. Uberoi's classes continue to be as popular as ever and comprise pupils from all over India and abroad.

Nimmi Uberoi, Pritam Uberoi's daughter, has rendered invaluable assistance, with her excellent professional expertise in cookery. She has helped in organising a variety of cookery programmes and demonstrations. She has won many awards of Canning and Preservation from the Government of India.

NON-VEGETARIAN
INDIAN COOKERY

Published by
Sterling Publishers Private Limited

NON-VEGETARIAN INDIAN COOKERY

PRITAM UBEROI
&
NIMMI UBEROI

A Sterling Paperback

STERLING PAPERBACKS
An imprint of
Sterling Publishers (P) Ltd.
L-10, Green Park Extension, New Delhi-110016
Ph.: 6511784, 6511785 Fax: 91-11-6851028

Non-Vegetarian Indian Cookery
©1992, Pritam Uberoi & Nimmi Uberoi
ISBN 81 207 1408 3
First Edition 1982
Reprint 1983, 1984, 1985, 1986, 1988, 1990
Second Revised Editon 1992
Reprint 1993, 1995, 1996, 1997, 1999

All rights are reserved. No part of this publication may be reproduced, stored in a retrieval system or transmitted, in any form or by any means, mechanical, photocopying, recording or otherwise, without prior written permission of the publisher.

Published by Sterling Publishers Pvt. Ltd., New Delhi-110016.
Lasertypeset at Vikas Compographics, New Delhi.
Printed at Ram Printograph, New Delhi.
Cover Printed at Elegant Printers, New Delhi.
Cover design by Imroz

INTRODUCTION

For the last thirty-five years I have devoted myself to lecturing and teaching in colleges, in public halls for charity programmes and held many demonstrations in the art of cooking. At the request of many hundreds of my pupils and well-wishers, I have ventured on a task which I sincerely hope will be of material benefit not only to Indian housewives but also to housewives abroad. Practically every recipe in this book is one that can be used in any country by the ordinary housewife.

In my childhood I can remember that I took eager interest in cooking with my mother. I had my education at Mahila Mahavidyalaya College, Lahore, and subsequently at Lady Irwin College, Delhi. I married Shri G.S. Uberoi, a Sikh businessman, in 1943. He is very fond of good food and in fact, has always been encouraging me to try new dishes which helped me immensely at the later stage. Mrs Tara Bari, ex-Director of Lady Irwin College, asked me to part with my knowledge of cooking for the benefit of the students of Lady Irwin College. I made quick progress and my dedication resulted in my selection as Director, Delhi School of Cookery. Although an introvert by nature and religious by views, I have ambitious plans of transforming young girls into accomplished wives in the society and endear them to their husbands. For, I am convinced, to use a cliche, that the easy way to a man's heart is through the stomach. It is a universal truth unchanged by time. A good kitchen at home prevents many tensions of marital life, destroys the temptation to 'eat out' at the restaurants, thereby providing an economic solution to many household problems, in addition to healthy nourishment.

My preparations of Western dishes have been admired by connoisseurs. My specially prepared dishes were displayed at the 15th World Vegetarian Conference held at Delhi in 1957 which were highly appreciated by press and the public. There my eldest daughter Jasmin (at that time just fourteen) was awarded first prize for salad preparation. My younger daughter Nimmi, also got first prize in canning and preservation from the Government of India, Community Canning and Preservation Centre. My children, one son and two daughters, have always provided constructive criticism on numerous culinary experiments in my kitchen. I am highly grateful to them. Finally I also wish to thank all those who have encouraged me in writing the non-vegetarian and vegetarian cookbooks.

B-5/5, Safdarjang Enclave, **Pritam Uberoi**
New Delhi-110029

CONTENTS

Introduction *v*
Glossary *xiii*
Dictionary of Cookery Words *xvi*
List of Kitchen Utensils *xviii*
Weights and Measures *xxi*
Important Hints *xxii*

1. **PULAO AND BIRIANI** 1
   Chicken Pulao
   Chicken Biriani
   Roasted Stuffed Chicken with Cheese and Mushroom Biriani
   Cheese and Mushroom Biriani for Roasted Stuffed Chicken
   Shahi Korma Chicken Pulao
   Egg Threads Fried Rice
   Fish Pulao
   Fish Kababs Pulao
   Akbari Mutton Pulao
   Keema Pulao
   Mutton Biriani
   Mutton Pulao
   Shah Jahani Biriani
   Pork Pulao
   Cocktail Prawn Kababs Pulao
   Prawn Pulao
   Teetar (Teal) Biriani

2. **STUFFED PARATHA AND PURI** 10
   Stuffed Keema or Minced Meat Paratha
   Chicken and Egg Paratha
   Egg Paratha
   Nan
   Keema Nan
   Stuffed Keema Puri
   Stuffed Spinach and Egg Puri
   Tomato and Cheese Pizza (Italian Style)

3. **CURRIES** 15
   Egg Omelette Curry
   Egg Shahi Omelette Curry
   Stuffed Egg Curry
   Brain Curry (Irani Style)
   Brain Curry (Punjabi Style)
   Akbari Chicken Curry
   Cream Chicken and Egg
   Chicken Jhal Fraize
   Embassy Chicken Curry
   Goanese Chicken Curry

Kashmiri Chicken Curry
Chicken Masala Curry
Mughlai Makhani Chicken Curry
Makhani Chicken Curry
Murg Musulam
Nargasi Chicken Curry
Tandoori Roasted Chicken Curry
Tandoori Mixed Grill
Roasted Teetar
Bengali Fish Curry
Fish Keema Curry
Kashmiri Fish Curry
Mughlai Fish Curry
Fish Kofta Curry
Plum Fish Kofta Curry
Stuffed Fish Tomato Curry
Fish Vindaloo Curry
Afghani Mutton Curry
Dalwala Meat
Dahiwala Meat
Goanese Mutton Curry
Kidney Korma
Irani Mutton Curry
Mutton Do Piaza
Mutton Magaj Curry
Multani Meat Curry
Minced Meat with Paneer Curry
Mutton Vindaloo Curry
Stuffed Cauliflower with Minced Meat
Shahi Korma
Mutton Rolls in Tomato Sauce
Roasted Mutton Leg

Rogan Josh
Stuffed Keema Tomato Curry
Cream Kofta Curry
Nargasi Kofta Curry
Panjabi Kofta Curry
Plum Kofta Curry
Mutton and Egg Kofta Curry
Bhuni Kaleji (Fried Liver)

4. **KABABS**   **43**

Egg Kababs
Brain Kababs
Bread Kababs with Fried Vegetables
Cocktail Fish Kababs
Fish Cakes or Kababs
Fish Roll
Fish Seekh Kababs
Fish Kababs
Fish Cream Pears
Cocktail Shami Kababs
Barrah Kababs
Boti Kababs
Hussani Kababs
Kashmiri Kababs
Nargasi Kababs
Shami Kababs
Seekh Kababs
Shikam Puri Kababs
Potato Kababs Stuffed with Meat
Mutton Kababs
Pork Seekh Kababs
Liver Kababs

5. **CHOPS AND TIKKAS**   **54**

Fish Chops
Dahi Chops

Goanese Mutton Chops
Mutton Chops
Mutton Chops with Gravy
Mughlai Chops
Sindhi Chops
Fried Pork Chops
Multani Chops
Chops in Tomato
Chicken Tikka
Fish Tikka
Mutton Tikka
Pork Tikka

6. **PAKORAS**   **60**
Chicken Pakora
Egg Pakora
Brain Pakora
Fish Pakora

7. **SNACKS**   **62**
Mutton Samosas
Meat Pie
Fish Rolls
Goanese Fish in Tomato Sauce
Fried Fish (Punjabi Style)
Fried Fish with Spices
Stuffed Pomfret
Stuffed Tomato with Fish
Tandoori Fish
Tomato Fish
Ham and Potato Balls
Fried Sausages
Stuffed Potato Sausages
Chicken Pickle
Meat Pickle
Cheese Toast

Egg in Tomato on Toast
Scrambled Eggs on Toast
Cheese Omelette Souffle
Egg Open Sandwiches (Russian Style)
Russian Sandwiches

8. **INDIAN PUDDINGS** **72**
Bread Pudding
Egg Halwa
Jalebi Pudding
Indian Royal Pudding
Rice Pudding
Shahi Tukri with Egg

9. **SOUPS**   **75**
Almond Soup with Clear Stock
Clear Soup
Chicken Cream Soup
French Onion Soup
Tomato Soup with Cream
Tomato Soup (Ukrainian Style)

10. **CHICKEN, FISH, MUTTON, PORK PREPARATIONS** **79**
Chicken
Grill Chicken
Chicken Chops
Fried Spinach
Fried Beans
Chicken a-la-King
Chicken a-la-Kiev
Chicken a-la-Mexicano
American Chicken
Chicken Maryland
Baked Cream Chicken

with Vegetables
Baked Chicken (Ukrainian Style)
Chicken Sandwiches
Club Sandwiches
Chicken Shashlik
Chicken Toast (French Style)
Chicken Omelette Souffle

Fish
Fish Baked with Noodles
Fried Sole Fish
Fish Cutlets
Fish Souffle
Hollandaise Sauce
Spaghetti with Meat Balls in Tomato Sauce
Fish Cream Pears
Fried Fish with Mushrooms (Thailand)
Fish with Rice (Damascus Style)
Baked Fish (Greek Style)
Fish Fingers
Baked Fish with Cheese

Mutton
Mutton Cutlets
Roasted Mutton Leg
Minced Meat and Potato Pears
Pate de Foie Gras Cocktail (Fench Style)
Brain Cutlets

Meat Pie
Mutton Pizza
Ashak (Afghanistan Style)
Stuffed Capsicums (Arabic Style)
Liver Toast
Scrambled Eggs with Ham on Toast
Ham Omelette Souffle

Pork
Grilled Pork Chops
Stuffed Eggs
Pork Shashlik
Ham and Pineapple Loaf
Fried Pork Chops
Egg Nun Style
Sausages with Spaghetti
Fried Sausages (Italian Style)
Ham Sandwiches
Magic Sausage Rolls

11. PUDDINGS AND ICE CREAMS   104

Puddings
Apple Tart
Bread Pudding (Italian Style)
Banana Trifle Pudding
Banana Pudding (Swedish Style)
Baked Coconut Custard
Caramel Custard
Cold Chocolate Cream Pudding
Chocolate Bread Pudding

Cold Chocolate Pudding (Italian Style)
Custard Pie
Cold Orange Pudding
Christmas Pudding
Embassy Special Pudding
Fruit Pudding with Custard
Fruit Gateux Pudding (French Style)
Hot Peaches Pudding
Hot Souffle
Lemon Pudding
Iceberg or Floating Pudding
Magic Bread Pudding
Meringue Lemon Pie
Orange Souffle
Orange Basket Pudding
Peach Berdoer
Steamed Fruit Custard
Singapore Souffle
Ice Creams
Almond Caramel Ice Cream
Banana Ice Cream
Banana Ice Cream (Italian Style)
Lemon and Vanilla Ice Cream (French)
Mango Ice Cream
Pista Ice Cream
Rainbow Ice Cream

12. **BISCUITS, PASTRIES AND CAKES   122**
Biscuits
Almond Biscuits
Almond Cookies
Cherry Dream Cookies
Cashewnut or Almond Biscuits
Fancy Biscuits
Fancy Chocolate Cream Biscuits
Lemon and Almond Cookies
Lemon Peels Biscuits
Lemon Wafers
Banana Fritters
Doughnuts
Pastry and Cake
Coffee Pastry
Dry Coconut Pastry
Jam Tart
Strawberry Pastry with Decoration
Swiss Rolls
Lemon Tart
Chocolate Almond Sticks Cake
Fancy Coconut Cake
Lemon and Chocolate Cake
Lemon Loaf Cake
Plain Fruit Cake
Plum Cake
Queen's Cake
Small Fancy Cake
Spiced Fruit Cake
Strawberry Cake with Decoration
White Fruit Cake
Mango Bread
Walnut Decorated Cake

GLOSSARY

English	Hindustani
Almond	*Badam*
Alum	*Phitcari*
Aniseed	*Saunf*
Apricots	*Khurmani*
Asafoetida	*Heeng*
Baking powder	*Pakane ka soda*
Bay leaf	*Tej patta*
Beans	*Same*
Beetroot	*Chukander*
Black pepper	*Kali mirchi*
Brinjal	*Baingan*
Buttermilk	*Lassi, Ghol*
Cabbage	*Bandh gobhi*
Capsicum	*Simla mirchi, Bara mirchi*
Cardamom	*Elaichi*
Carrot	*Gajar*
Castor sugar	*Powder or Pisi cheenee*
Cashewnuts	*Kaju*
Carraway	*Ajwain*
Cayenne	*Lal mirchi*
Cauliflower	*Phool gobhi*
Cheese	*Vilayti paneer*
Chillies	*Lal mirchi*
Cinnamon	*Dalchini*
Citric acid	*Tatri*
Cloves	*Laung*
Cooking apple	*Kaccha seb*
Cochineal	*Meetha gulabi rang*
Coconut	*Narial*
Colocasia	*Arabi*
Coriander leaves	*Hara dhania*
Coriander seeds	*Sukha dhania*

Cucumber	*Kheera*
Cuminseeds	*Zeera*
Curd	*Dahi*
Dates	*Khajur*
Drumsticks	*Saijan ki phali*
Dried ginger	*Sonth*
Dry breadcrumbs	*Sookhi double roti ka choora*
Dry mango	*Amchoor*
Fenugreek	*Methi*
Flour	*Maida*
Beans leaves	*Pharas beans*
French mint	*Hara pudina*
Garlic	*Lehsoon*
Ghee	*Clarified butter*
Ginger	*Adarak*
Gram	*Chana*
Gram dal	*Chana ki dal*
Gram flour	*Besan*
Grapes	*Angoor*
Green chilli	*Hara mirch*
Green pumpkin	*Ghia, louki, kaddu*
Griddle	*Tawa*
Groundnut oil	*Moongphali oil*
Icing sugar	*Icing cheenee*
Jaggery	*Gur*
Kewara flavour	*Indian kewara essence diluted with water*
Khoya	*Milk solidified by prolonged cooking*
Lady'sfinger	*Bhindi*
Lemon	*Neembu*
Lemon rind	*Neembu ka chhilka*
Lentils	*Dal*
Mace	*Jawitri*
Macaroni	*It is prepared from flour and forced through tubes*
Mango	*Aam*
Mustard	*Rai*
Mustard oil	*Sarson oil*
Nutmeg	*Jaiphal*

Onion	Pyaz
Onion seeds	Kalaunji
Papaya	Papita
Peas	Mutta
Peppercorn	Sabat kali mirch
Peaches	Aalu
Pickle	Achar
Pistachio	Pista
Pomegranate	Anardana
Poppy seeds	Khus khus
Raddish	Mooli
Raisins	Kismis
Red chilli powder	Kashmiri mirch powder
Rice	Chawal
Rose water	Gulab jal
Saffron	Kesar
Salt	Namak
Sesamum	Til
Semolina	Sooji, Rawa
Soft breadcrumbs	Taji double roti ka choora
Spinach	Palak
Spring onion	Hara pyaz
Sugar	Cheenee
Sultana	Munakka (bara kismis)
Sweet potato	Shakarkandi
Tamarind	Imli
Turnip	Shulgum
Turmeric	Huldi
Thymol seeds	Ajwain
Vinegar	Sirka
White gram	Kabuli chana
White pumpkin	Petha
Wholewheat flour	Gehun ka atta

DICTIONARY OF COOKERY WORDS

Bake	To cook by dry heat in an oven or tandoor (Indian oven).
Batter	A mixture of flour and water or milk, thin enough to pour.
Beat	A mix with a vigorous over and over motion with spoon, wire beater or egg beater. To enclose air in the food.
Blanch	To remove skins from fruit or nuts by dipping into boiling water.
Blend	To mix the ingredients very thoroughly.
Boil	To cook in boiling water or any other liquid in which bubbles are breaking on the surface and steam is given off.
Brush	To spread thinly.
Caramel syrup	Melt sugar to a brown colour on fire and add a little water. It is only used for colouring and flavouring.
Chill	To allow to become thoroughly cold but not frozen.
Chop	To cut into very small pieces with a sharp knife or chopper.
Cream together	To mix two ingredients together such as creaming butter or ghee with sugar until the mixture is light and fluffy.
Deep frying	To cook in hot ghee or oil deep enough to float the stuff.
Dissolve	To cause the dry ingredients to transform into liquid.

Dust	To sprinkle or coat lightly with flour.
Fold in	To mix by a gentle motion. Proper folding in prevents loss of air.
Garnish	To decorate.
Ghee	Clarified butter.
Grate	To grind into shreds or particles.
Mince	To cut with a sharp knife into very small pieces.
Peel	To remove outside covering by stripping off as from peaches, tomatoes etc.
Sift	To pass through a sieve.
Simmer	To cook in water on very slow fire below boiling point.
Stir	To mix with spoon using circular motion.
Fondant	Sugar syrup cooked to a soft ball stage, cooled and kneaded to creamy mass.
Shallow frying	To cook in small amount of ghee.
Soak	To immerse in liquid for a time.
Whip	To beat rapidly.

LIST OF KITCHEN UTENSILS

2 or 3 sharp knives—for paring and cutting vegetables. Bread knife with saw tooth edge for cutting bread and sandwiches.
2 wooden spoons—for mixing puddings, cakes and curd.
3 kitchen spoons ⎫
2 teaspoons   ⎬ for general use.
1 tablespoon   ⎭
1 pair of tongs.
1 set of rolling pin and board for chapatties, parathas, biscuits etc.
1 chopping board—to cut vegetable on it.
1 apple corer—To make holes in apples or other fruits and remove the cores.
6 containers with lids—preferably a set in which each fits into another for convenience in storing.
6 griddles (*tawa*)—for baking chapatties and parathas.
1 frying pan—for shallow frying.
1 karahi—a deep pan for frying solids in deep fat (oil or ghee).
1 skimmer—janjara or pauni (large spoon with holes for taking out fried food out of the hot ghee.)
1 grater (Ghia-Kus)—to shred food into tiny particles.
1 pancake turner or spatula—for turning and basting solids with a long handle.
1 grinding stone (a slab and a muller)—for grinding solids to a paste or for grating to a pulp.
1 funnel—for filling bottles.
1 lemon squeezer—for extracting juice from lemons.
1 tin opener
1 bottle opener
1 cork screw

1 gravy strainer—for soups.
Thali—generally flat and round plate.
1 sieve—for sifting flour.
2 vegetable strainers.
Pint measure for measuring liquids.
6 mixing bowls—a set of convenient sizes.
1 ground spices box.
1 set of scales.
2 cake tins (round and square).
Biscuit cutter.
1 jelly mould.
2 pie dishes.
Parat or thali—large metal plate for kneading flour.
1 masher machine for mashing vegetables.
2 buckets.
1 large vessel for storing water for cooking purposes.
2 sigris or chulha (Indian stoves).
1 kerosene oil stove.
1 oven (Indian made).
1 fork.
1 metal strainer.
6 dusters for straining milk.
Egg beater—for whipping cream.
Wire beater—for beating mixture.
Wire rack—for cooking cakes, biscuits and bread.
1 meat safe.
1 kettle.
Ice box for chilling the food.
1 teacup for measuring the liquid.
Sugar canisters or sugar pot.
Flour crock.
Tandoor—a rural oven, made of straw reinforced clay, in the shape of a barrel. It has a wide opening at the top through which ignited fuel is introduced, and a small opening at the base for circulation of air and removal of ashes. When the inner walls are red hot, the food to be cooked is suspended inside the tandoor for baking by radiant heat. Chapatties or nans, however, are pressed against the inner walls.

WEIGHTS AND MEASURES

Household measures by cups and spoons are more convenient and are easily available. Three precautions have to be taken while measuring:

(i) Fill the cup with dry ingredients and pass the edge of a knife over the top to level off.
(ii) Measure the sifted flour. The cup should not be packed tightly.
(iii) Melt the ghee and then measure it. One measuring cup weighs approximately eight ozs.

Equivalents

2 ozs	1 chatak
2 lbs	1 seer
1 pint	20 ozs
$1/2$ pint	10 ozs
4 teacups	1 pint
2 measuring cups	1 pint
1 lb milk (liquid)	2 measuring cups
1 lb sugar	$2^1/_2$ measuring cups
1 lb dry fruit (chopped)	3 measuring cups
2 pints (40 ozs)	1 quart
1 teacup full of water or milk	5 ozs
60 drops	1 teaspoon
2 teaspoons	1 dessertspoon
3 teaspoons	1 tablespoon
2 tablespoons	1 oz
1 tumbler	6 ozs

IMPORTANT HINTS

Instead of ghee any kind of fat can be used such as dripping, lard, margarine, suet or any edible oil.

Garlic powder can be used instead of fresh garlic. $1/4$ teaspoon garlic powder is equal to 4 garlic flakes.

$1/2$ tin spinach is equal to 2 lbs spinach.

1 teaspoon dry ginger is equal to 2 teaspoons fresh ginger (but soak dry ginger powder in $1/4$ cup of water).

Curries should always be cooked slowly to extract all the richness and flavour of the spices.

Don't use soda bicarbonate for boiling vegetables as it destroys the vitamins.

Don't use large amounts of water for cooking vegetables.

Scrape the skins of the vegetables and don't peel them deeply as Mrs Peeler is the vitamin stealer.

Cook fleshy food on slow fire till tender. Excessive cooking destroys the food value.

PULAO AND BIRIANI

CHICKEN PULAO
serves 6

- 1/2 medium sized chicken
- 6 cups stock
- 1 big onion
- 15 almonds
- 6 green cardamoms
- 2 tsps white cuminseeds
- salt to taste
- 3 small pieces of ginger
- 1/2 kg rice
- 1/2 cup ghee
- 15 gms sultana
- 4 cloves
- 1 small piece of cinnamon
- 2 hard boiled eggs
- 1/4 tsp saffron
- 1/2 tsp red chilli powder

Wash and soak rice for 15 minutes. Cut chicken into medium pieces and then cook it with ginger, salt, whole spices, 2 1/2 lbs water, cuminseeds tied in muslin cloth until tender. Throw away the spices from the stock. Fry onion slices until light brown and then fry boiled chicken pieces for a few minutes. Add stock, rice, red chilli powder, salt and saffron dissolved in a little hot water and cook until rice is tender and each grain is separate. Garnish with hard boiled eggs cut into round slices and golden brown almonds and sultanas. Serve hot.

CHICKEN BIRIANI

See the recipe of Mutton Biriani.
Same recipe as for mutton biriani. Omit mutton and add small chicken pieces.

ROASTED STUFFED CHICKEN WITH CHEESE & MUSHROOM BIRIANI
serves 6

- 1 chicken
- 1 small onion
- 3/4 cup ghee
- 25 gms garlic
- 2 big pieces of fresh ginger

½ tsp saffron
2 bay leaves
½ tsp nutmeg
10 peppercorns
¼ cup coconut
1 cup curd
small raw papaya

4 tsps dry coriander
1 small piece of mace
4 cloves
6 green cardamoms
2 tsps poppy seeds
225 gms onion
salt and red chilli powder to taste

Prick the chicken with a sharp knife. Crush garlic and then in it add salt and 3 cups of water and wash the chicken with it. Dry with duster. Peel raw papaya and grind it with salt and then rub it on chicken and keep aside. Grind all the ingredients except the ½ lb (225 gms) of onion, bay leaves, cardamoms and saffron to a fine paste. Cut the onion into rings and fry until light brown. Remove the onion from ghee, cool a little, then crush between your palms and mix with the masala paste. In the same ghee (left over from frying onions) add bay leaves, whole cardamoms and the masala paste, curd and salt and fry well till the ghee separates from the masala. Stuff the chicken with half of the masala. Dissolve saffron in a little hot water, then add into the rest of the masala. Place the chicken on the masala, add enough water and cover the degchi and cook it on slow fire until tender. Add a few drops of kewara flavour. Remove from fire. Untruss the chicken and dish it on a bed of cheese and mushroom biriani and then pour over thick gravy. Serve hot at dinner or lunch party.

CHEESE AND MUSHROOM BIRIANI FOR ROASTED STUFFED CHICKEN

serves 6

½ kg rice (salha basmati)
2 bay leaves
Coarsely ground spices:
    4 cloves, 3 tsps white cuminseeds, 2 pieces of cinnamon, 4 green cardamoms
1 cup milk
1 tsp kewara flavour
salt to taste

water (6 cups)
1 big onion
½ tsp red chilli powder
225 gms cheese
½ cup ghee
4 silver leaves
1 carrot
28 gms black mushroom
½ kg peas

Soak mushroom in water overnight. Soak rice for about two hours, fry small pieces of cheese in ghee till light brown. Fry chopped onion and bay leaves. Add water and salt and boil. Now add rice, chopped carrot, peas, chopped mushrooms and ground spices. Cook till water is absorbed and each grain is separated. Mix kewara flavour and decorate with stuffed chicken. (If rice is not tender then cover it with wet cloth and put on low heat.)

SHAHI KORMA CHICKEN PULAO   serves 6

1/2 medium sized chicken
6 cups stock
2 tsps ground dry coriander
1 tsp ground cuminseeds
6 green cardamoms
1/2 cup ghee
55 gms cashewnuts
1 tomato
1/2 kg rice
3/4 cup curd
1/4 tsp ground cloves
1 small piece of cinnamon (ground)
1 onion
1/3 tsp grated nutmeg
1/2 tsp red chilli powder
salt to taste

Fry medium pieces of boiled chicken with ground spices, whole cardamoms until golden brown. Add curd, red chilli powder and chopped tomato without skin and stir for a few minutes. Add soaked rice, salt and stock and grated nutmeg and cook until tender, and water is evaporated. Garnish with fried and crisp onion rings and lightly roasted cashewnuts.

EGG THREADS FRIED RICE   serves 6

1/2 kg rice
1/2 tsp chilli powder
2 tsps ground spices (4 cloves, 1/2 tsp white cuminseeds, 1 small piece of cinnamon, 2 big cardamoms)
5 cups water
2 carrots
1 onion
1 or 2 bay leaves
4 eggs
1/2 cup ghee
4 or 5 tbsps ghee
salt to taste

Wash and soak rice for 15 minutes. Fry onion, bay leaves in ghee till brown. Add water, chilli powder, ground spices, salt, long strips of carrot and rice and cook until the rice has absorbed all the water and each grain is separate and then remove from fire.

Egg Threads

Beat eggs lightly with $3/4$ tsp salt. Heat the ghee in frying pan, then spread a little beaten egg over it and brown slightly both sides of it. Cut the thin omelette into narrow and long strips. Repeat the process until all the eggs are used up. Decorate the rice with these fried egg threads.

FISH PULAO   serves 6

680 gms fish without bones
5 cups water
$1/2$ tsp red chilli powder
salt to taste
3 tsps lemon juice
170 gms onion
2 big black cardamoms
$1/2$ tsp aniseed
ghee for shallow frying

$3/4$ cup curd
$1/2$ kg rice
$1/2$ cup ghee
4 colves
1 one-inch stick of cinnamon
5 garlic cloves
4 tsps cuminseeds
55 gms besan

Pick, wash and soak rice for 35 minutes. Wash the small pieces of fish and then dry them, then rub lemon juice and salt on them. Grind cuminseeds and aniseeds and then mix into besan. Dust the fish with it and keep aside for a few minutes. Fry in shallow ghee until nicely browned. Fry onion with whole spices in 8 oz ghee until light brown and then stir in ground garlic until brown. Add rice, water, salt, curd and red chilli powder and cook on medium fire until rice absorbs all the water and is thoroughly cooked; each grain should be separate. Finally mix fried fish into the rice.

FISH KABABS PULAO   serves 6

$1/2$ kg rice
6 cups fish stock
3 ground cloves

1 big onion
salt to taste
$1/2$ tsp red chilli powder

1 tsp white cuminseeds
2 big cardamoms
   (ground)

½ tsp cinnamon
½ cup ghee

Fish Kababs

½ kg fish
4 small ginger pieces
2 green chillies
salt to taste
2 egg whites

1½ tsp ground spices
1 small onion
¾ tsp black pepper
ghee or deep frying

Boil fish in 2¼ lbs water with one tsp salt until tender. Take out the fish pieces from stock. Cool them, remove bones and skin and then mash them. Mix in ground spices, salt, chopped green chilli, ginger and onion and mix well. Now make small rounds and dip in lightly beaten whites of egg. Fry in hot ghee until light brown. Drain on paper. Soak rice for 15 mts. Now cut the onion into thin slices and fry in ghee until brown. Add fish stock, salt, chilli powder, ground cuminseeds, cinnamon, cardamoms, cloves and rice. Cook until tender. Remove from fire and on the rice place the fried fish balls, cover the vessel for 15 minutes. Serve hot.

AKBARI MUTTON PULAO   serves 6

½ kg rice
6 cups stock
1 small piece of ginger
1 onion
2 tsps spices
1 bay leaf
4 cloves

½ kg lean mutton
½ tsp red chilli powder
5 garlic cloves
85 gms sultana
salt to taste
1 small piece of cinnamon
1 tsp black corns

Wash and soak rice for 15 minutes. Boil mutton with bay leaf, cinnamon, peppercorn, cloves, ginger and garlic until tender. Throw away the spices, ginger and garlic. Fry chopped onion until light brown. Add boiled mutton, red chilli powder, salt and ground spices, stock, rice and cook on medium fire till stock is evaporated. Mix fried raisins and cook on very slow fire till tender and each rice grain is separate. Serve hot. (If stock is less than 2 lbs. add hot water to it.)

KEEMA PULAO
serves 6

$1/2$ kg rice
225 gms thick minced mutton
2 tsps white cuminseeds (ground)
1 small piece of cinnamon
4 cloves

6 cups water
1 onion
1 bay leaf
$1/4$ tsp red chilli powder
$1/2$ cup ghee
6 green cardamoms
salt to taste

Heat ghee, add thick minced meat, 2 cups water, whole cloves, cardamoms, ground cuminseeds, cinnamon and bay leaf and cook until minced meat is dry. Add soaked rice, salt, red chilli powder and water and cook on medium fire until tender and water is evaporated. Each grain of rice should be separated. Cut onion into rings and fry until nice browned and crisp and then garnish the pulao with it. Serve hot.

MUTTON BIRIANI
serves 6

$1/2$ kg mutton
water to cover the meat
3 cloves
2 small pieces of cinnamon
6 green cardamoms
1 small garlic pod
1 tsp aniseed
$1/2$ cup ghee
20 black peppercorns
$1 1/2$ tsp white cuminseed
$1/4$ tsp nutmeg

$1/2$ kg rice
3 bay leaves
5 tsps stock for rice
2 big cardamoms
$3/4$ tsp orange colour
$3 1/2$ tsps whole dry coriander
2 tsps kewara flavour
salt to taste
4 pieces ginger
1 onion

Boil meat with garlic pod and all the spices except nutmeg and tie in cloth aniseeds and dry coriander and cook until tender. Fry onion and add meat and fry for 5 minutes. Add soaked rice, strained stock and $1/2$ tsp orange colour and cook until water has evaporated, add grated nutmeg, kewara flavour and mix well. Mix remaining $1/4$ tsp orange colour with half of the rice and keep the vessel covered for 2 minutes. Serve at dinner or lunch.

MUTTON PULAO   serves 6

$1/2$ kg rice
$1/2$ cup ghee
6 small slices of fresh ginger
28 or 56 gms flour (or 4 or 6 tsps)
2 hard boiled eggs
2 tsps white cuminseeds
A few drops of orange colour
5 cups stock

1 kg lean mutton
2 tsps dry coriander
1 piece cinnamon (about 1 inch)
1 tsp ground spices
$1/2$ tsp peppercorns
2 tsps ground spices
3 cloves
113 gms onion
salt to taste

Pick, wash and soak rice for 10 minutes. Fry onion in 2 oz ghee until light brown, then stir in it ground ginger, ground coriander, pepper corns and meat for a few minutes. Add enough water and cook until meat is tender. Take out the meat pieces from the stock. Rub salt and ground spices on meat pieces, dust with flour and fry in shallow ghee. Heat $1/2$ cup ghee and fry cloves, cinnamon and then add 5 cups stock, salt and rice and cook until $3/4$ cooked. Remove from fire. Mix orange colour into half rice and then mix meat. Put them in another vessel and cover it with a wet cloth. Put lid on it and heat it on a very slow fire until tender.

SHAH JAHANI BIRIANI   serves 6

$1/2$ kg rice
2 big cardamoms
1 garlic pod
1 cinnamon ($1/2$ inch)
2 tsps aniseeds
2 tsps coriander leaves (tie them in a muslin cloth)

5 big cups stock
3 green cardamoms
1 big piece of ginger (about 1 inch)
4 cloves
1 tsp red chilli powder
2 tsps coriander leaves
2 tsps kewara flavour
3 tsps salt
1 medium sized onion

1 medium sized onion (slices long and thin)
1 kitchen tbsp ghee
4 or 5 cashewnuts or almonds
$1/4$ tsp orange colour
$1/2$ kg mutton ribs
$1/4$ tsp grated nutmeg
2 tsps ground cuminseed
1 cup milk
$1/4$ tsp yellow colour
1 or 2 bay leaves
silver leaves for decoration
$3/4$ cup ghee

Boil the meat with 3 tsps salt, garlic pod, big piece of ginger, clove, cinnamon, big cardamoms, green cardamoms and the muslin cloth containing aniseeds and coriander seeds and 10 cups of water till it becomes tender. Then put it on the strainer and remove the whole spices, garlic pod and the muslin bag. Soak the rice for 20 minutes. Then fry the long slices of onion in ghee with bay leaf till light brown. Add stock, ground white cuminseed, salt, red chilli powder, fried cashewnuts (cut into half) and mutton ribs and cook till it boils. Add milk and then soaked rice and mix them well. Then cook it and don't stir till the water is evaporated. Put it on a very slow fire till rice becomes tender. Then mix grated nutmeg and kewara flavour. Pour the colours separately with a tsp on the rice and keep for a few minutes. Remove from the fire and keep it for 10 minutes. Put it on an oval shaped dish and decorate it with silver leaves.

PORK PULAO

Same recipe as for mutton pulao. Omit mutton and add pork. Use only 2 oz (56 gms) ghee in pork pulao.

COCKTAIL PRAWN KABABS PULAO serves 6

$1/2$ kg rice
$1/4$ tsp ground cinnamon
$1/4$ tsp ground big cardamom
1 small piece mace
$1/2$ cup ghee
6 cups water
$1/4$ tsp ground cloves
2 tsp ground white cuminseeds
salt to taste
56 gms cashewnuts

Cocktail Prawn Kababs

225 gms cleaned prawns
2 green chillies
1 tsp chopped coriander leaves

3 small onions
1 tsp ground spices
½ tsp chilli powder
salt to taste

Wash and dry prawns and then mince them. Mix one chopped onion, green chillies, salt and ground spices into minced prawns. Make small round balls the then put in 2 lb boiling water for five to ten minutes. Remove from water and then fry until light brown in shallow ghee. Fry slices of two onions until light brown, add soaked rice, ground spices, red chilli powder, salt and water of boiled prawn kababs and cook until water is absorbed and each grain is separate. Garnish the rice with fried cashew nuts and fried prawn kababs.

PRAWN PULAO
serves 6

½ kg rice
170 gms cleaned prawns
2 tsps poppy seeds
1 onion
salt to taste

6 cups stock
25 gms fresh coconut
2 small pieces of ginger
½ tsp red chilli powder
½ cup ghee

Soak rice for 10 minutes. Boil prawns with ginger in 2 lb salted water until tender. Throw away the ginger from the stock. Fry onion slices until light brown and mix ground paste of coconut, poppy seeds, cardamoms and cuminseeds and fry for five minutes. Add boiled prawns, rice stock, salt and red chilli powder, cook until tender and water is absorbed. Serve hot.

TEETAR (TEAL) BIRIANI

Same recipe as for roasted stuff chicken in cheese and mushroom biriani. Here stuff two teals with one chicken's stuffing.

STUFFED PARATHA AND PURI

STUFFED KEEMA OR MINCED MEAT PARATHA *serves 8*

Filling

1/4 kg keema
   (minced meat)
few coriander leaves
2 garlic flakes
salt to taste
2 green chillies
1 cup water
1 tsp ginger
2 tsps ground cuminseeds

Cook minced meat with water, chopped ginger and garlic till tender and dry. Mix chopped green chillies, coriander leaves, ground cumin and salt. Fill it in parathas.

Covering

3 cups wheat flour
3 tsp ghee
water for kneading
1/2 tsp salt
1 cup melted ghee

Knead sifted flour and salt with ghee and water into a soft dough, keep covered for 25 minutes. Divide into 8 portions. Press each portion in the centre and fill cooked minced meat, cover the filling entirely, seal well and flatten a little, roll into a chappati and fry on a tawa, using a little ghee till both sides are golden brown and crisp. Serve hot at breakfast or lunch with curd.

CHICKEN AND EGG PARATHA *serves 8*

3 cups whole wheat flour
1 cup ghee
1 level tsp salt

Chicken Mixture

2 chicken breasts
   (boiled and chopped)
9 coriander leaves
1 tsp ground cuminseeds
5 or 6 eggs
2 green chillies
salt to taste

Beat the egg in it, mix all the ingredients and keep aside.

Paratha Dough

Knead sifted flour and salt with a little water and 4 tsps ghee. Keep it covered with wet cloth for $1/2$ hour and again knead it into a soft dough. Take small portions of dough, roll them out into chappaties and smear with ghee. Fold them up again into round balls and roll out once more. Put each on a heavy and hot tawa, bake on one side of the paratha and turn it over. Add a little ghee from the sides till they become golden brown and crisp. Pour a little chicken mixture on top of the crisp paratha, then turn it and keep it till egg and chicken are set and golden brown in colour. Serve hot for breakfast.

EGG PARATHA *serves 6*

Same recipe as for Chicken and Egg Paratha. Only omit the chicken.

NAN *serves 8*

3 cups flour
1 cup wholewheat flour
1 tsp salt
$1^1/_2$ tsp soda bicarbonate
6 tsps melted ghee
2 tsps aniseeds
1 egg
3 tsps sugar
1 cup curd
$1/_4$ tsp onion seeds
water to knead the dough
2 tsps poppy seeds

Mix egg, salt, sugar, ghee and curd into sifted flour and wholewheat flour, knead it with a little water until smooth and elastic, keep it covered with wet cloth for $1/_2$ hour. In the meanwhile heat the tandoor. Dissolve soda in $1/_4$ cup of water, then mix into the dough and knead it. Make big 8 round balls. Wet the balls with a little melted ghee and beaten egg. Sprinkle aniseed, poppy seed and onion seed on the top of balls and make strips with the back of knife. Roll it round with wet hands and stretch it long, and place on moderate tandoor and cover tandoor till nan is golden brown. Remove from the tandoor and serve hot. If it cannot be served immediately wrap it in the duster so that it may not become hard. Serve it with tandoori chicken.

Note for Oven
Grease the baking tray and dust it with flour. Put the rolled nan with hand on the tray and bake in moderate oven (350°) till golden brown. Heat the oven for 10 minutes before baking.

KEEMA NAN
serves 8

Keema Mixture
1 cup minced meat
1 tsp coriander powder
1 yolk of egg
2 green chillies
salt to taste

Cook all the above except egg till tender and dry. Cool it, mix yolk of egg, keep it aside.

Nan Dough
3 cups flour
1 egg
1 tsp salt
6 tsps melted ghee
1½ tsps soda bicarbonate
1 cup wholewheat flour
3 tsps sugar
1 cup curd
Water to knead the dough

It is the same as for nan, only omit poppy seeds, aniseeds, and onion seeds. Spread keema mixed with a yolk of egg, serve it at lunch.

STUFFED KEEMA PURI
serves 6

Filling
1 cup minced meat
1 tsp ground cumin
1 tsp chopped ginger
2 green chillies
salt to taste
1 cup water

Cook all the above together till tender and dry. Keep aside.

Covering

2¼ cups wholewheat flour
¼ tsp salt

ghee for deep frying
6 tsps ghee

Sift flour and salt and knead it with water until smooth and a little stiff. Cover with wet cloth and keep it aside for 30 minutes. Knead it again and make small round balls about the size of a walnut. In it fill minced meat mixture and roll it ¼ inch thick and fry in hot ghee till it puffs up like a balloon and turns golden brown. Remove from ghee. Serve hot at breakfast or lunch.

STUFFED SPINACH AND EGG PURI   serves 6

Filling

250 gms spinach
2 green chillies chopped
salt to taste

1 full boiled egg
1 tsp coriander powder

Remove the stems from spinach. Wash and chop them. Cook in ¼ cup of water till tender and dry. Mash it, in it mix grated egg, green chilli, coriander powder and salt. Keep it aside.

Covering

The same as for Stuffed Keema Puri. Serve it at breakfast or lunch.

TOMATO AND CHEESE PIZZA
(Italian Style)   serves 6

1 packet of yeast
3½ cups flour
1 cup lukewarm water

½ level tsp salt
5 tsps ghee or any fat

Soak the yeast in lukewarm water for 10 minutes till dissolved. Sift flour and salt on wooden board and knead it with yeast mixture and ghee till smooth and elastic. Make into a ball and place it in big pan covered and let it rise in warm place for two hours till twice in bulk. Place it on a floured board and pound lightly to deflate it. Divide the dough into two equal parts and stretch each part on the bottom of a greased 12" pie dish and put the tomato filling and sprinkle cheese on it. Bake it in hot oven (400°F) for about 20 to 30 minutes.

Tomato Filling

$1/2$ kg tomatoes
1 tsp sugar
1 cup onion slices

$1/4$ tsp white pepper
salt to taste
$3/4$ cup grated cheese

Cook the chopped tomatoes till tender. Pass through a sieve. Mix salt, pepper, sugar, and cook till thick. Cool and spread on pizza dough, arrange onion slices and sprinkle cheese.

CURRIES

EGG OMELETTE CURRY *serves 8*

Omelette
6 eggs
salt to taste
2 green chillies
2 tsps ghee
a few green coriander leaves

Beat yolks, salt, chopped green chillies and coriander leaves. Whisk the white of egg to stiff froth and fold it lightly in the yolks. Melt ghee in frying pan or griddle and pour beaten eggs and stir on the surface until it begins to set. Leave until nicely browned underneath. Then slip a knife under it and fold first from one side and then from other towards the centre. Drain on paper and cut medium sized pieces. Serve at lunch or dinner.

Gravy
4 medium onions
14 gms ginger
170 gms tomatoes
1 tsp red chilli powder
salt to taste
1 tsp white cuminseeds
6 garlic flakes
$1/2$ tsp turmeric
a few coriander leaves
2 tsps ground spices
3 tbsps ghee

Fry chopped onion till golden brown, add ground ginger and garlic and stir until dry. Add ground cuminseeds, chopped tomatoes, salt, turmeric, red chilli powder and ground spices and stir it until it turns into a thick gravy. Add 3 cups of water and cook till one cup water is left, then cook omelette pieces in gravy.

EGG SHAHI OMELETTE CURRY *serves 6*

Same recipe as for omelette curry but only sprinkle melon seeds on the omelettes and then roll it. (Take $1/2$ cup melon seeds).

STUFFED EGG CURRY *serves 6*

6 boiled eggs
2 or 3 green chillies
½ cup milk
½ tsp ground spices
1 tsp ground cuminseeds
1 beaten egg
ghee for frying

340 gms spinach
2 or 3 green chillies
1 cup fresh crumbs (very fine)
few coriander leaves
dry breadcrumbs for coating

Remove the stems of spinach, wash and then chop it and cook till tender and dry. Then soak the fresh breadcrumbs in milk for 10 minutes. Cut the boiled eggs lengthwise and remove the yolks. Mix yolks, ground spices, cumin, few coriander leaves, green chillies, salt, and soaked breadcrumbs into cooked spinach. Then fill the egg white cases with spinach mixture. Dip into the beaten egg mixed with 3 tsps of water, coat them with breadcrumbs, then fry them till golden brown. And finally put them in the gravy at the time of serving.

Gravy

1 heaped cup of chopped onion
1 tsp ghee
6 garlic flakes
salt to taste

280 gms boiled tomatoes
1½ tsp ground spices
2 tsps ground ginger
1 tsp level red chilli powder
1½ tsp ground cuminseeds

Fry the onion till golden brown, add ground ginger, garlic and 1½ cups of water and cook till the water evaporates and the onions become tender. Add peeled and chopped tomatoes, ground spices, salt, red chilli powder, cumin and cook till it leaves its ghee. Add 2½ cups of water and cook till the gravy becomes thick. Put the stuffed eggs in the dish and then pour boiling gravy over it and garnish with a few coriander leaves.

BRAIN CURRY (Irani Style) *serves 6*

3 sheep's brains
10 garlic cloves
¼ tsp turmeric powder

2 big onions
1 tsp ground fresh ginger
½ tsp thin coconut milk

6 blanched almonds (slit in halves)
2 tomatoes
2 tsps ground spices
$1/8$ tsp grated nutmeg
salt to taste
3 tsps raisins
6 green cardamoms
170 gms ghee
4 tsps vinegar

Wash the brains thoroughly and then soak in fresh salted water for 35 minutes. Now cook them in sufficient water in which a little salt and 4 tsps vinegar have been added, until firm. Drain and cut into medium pieces. Fry ground onion till golden brown, add ground ginger and garlic and one cup of water till dry. Add peeled and chopped tomatoes, salt, green cardamoms, turmeric, chilli powder and stir until thick. Add boiled brains, almonds, cleaned raisins, coconut milk or juice and little water and cook on slow fire until gravy is thick. Mix ground spices, nutmeg and chopped coriander leaves and then remove from fire. Serve hot at lunch or dinner.

BRAIN CURRY (Punjabi Style) serves 6

2 sheep's brains
2 tsps ground cuminseed
$1/2$ tsp turmeric
1 cup curd
2 large tomatoes
salt to taste
1 large onion
2 tsps ground dry coriander
$1/2$ tsp red chilli powder
2 tsps lemon juice
$1/2$ cup ghee

Wash the brains thoroughly and then remove the skin. Soak it in fresh salted water for one hour. Now boil 3 cups of water with lemon juice and $1/2$ tsp salt in a pan and then in it cook brains until firm. Drain and cut into medium pieces. Fry chopped onion until golden brown, stir in turmeric, chopped and peeled tomatoes, salt, ground spices, red chilli powder and curd until thick gravy. Add the brains and a little water in which the brains have been boiled and cook on very slow fire for 10 minutes. Remove from fire, garnish with chopped coriander leaves. Serve hot at lunch or dinner.

AKBARI CHICKEN CURRY *serves 6*

1 medium sized chicken
56 gms ginger
2 bay leaves
3 tsps raisins
1 tsp red chilli powder
1 tsp ground spices
silver leaves for decoration

4 onions
8 green cardamoms
10 cloves of garlic
2 carrots
113 gms khoya
8 tsps cream
$1/2$ cup ghee

Fry ground onions with bay leaves and green cardamons until light brown. Add ground garlic, ginger, chilli powder, ground spices and salt and fry until gravy is thick. Add meat pieces and fry for a few minutes, add water and cook until meat is tender and dry. Add chopped and boiled carrot, raisins and again cook for a few minutes. Add mashed khoya and cream. Decorate with silver leaves and serve hot.

CREAM CHICKEN AND EGG *serves 4*

1 chicken breast
$1/2$ tsp level white pepper
3 tsps flour
$1/2$ cup cream
3 tsps butter
1 firm tomato
   (for decoration)

3 hard boiled eggs
$2 1/2$ tsps lemon juice
2 cups milk
salt to taste
3 tsps onion
1 bay leaf

Boil chicken with bay leaf till tender. Then remove bones and cut into small pieces. Melt butter, in it fry flour and onion for a few minutes. Then add milk and chicken pieces and cook for a few minutes. Now add cream and mix on the fire. Remove from fire, mix salt, lemon juice and small pieces of boiled eggs. Put them hot in the dish and then decorate them with tomato slices. Serve with bread slices.

CHICKEN JHAL FRAIZE *serves 4*

$1/2$ chicken
3 small fresh ginger slices
$1/2$ tomato

$1/2$ carrot
1 bay leaf
$1/2$ cup peas

2 green chillies
1 tsp ghee
1 onion
1 tsp chopped coriander leaves
1/4 tsp red chilli powder
1 boiled medium sized potato
1/4 tsp black pepper
1/4 tsp turmeric
salt to taste
2 tsps tomato ketchup

Boil chicken with carrot, peas, bay leaf and two ginger slices until tender, cool and remove the bones. Heat ghee, fry onion slices and chopped ginger until light brown. Add turmeric, salt, pepper, chopped green chillies, chilli powder, medium pieces of potato, chicken pieces, carrot, peas, coriander leaves and cook for a few minutes. Add tomato sauce and small pieces of tomato. Serve hot at lunch or dinner.

EMBASSY CHICKEN CURRY   *serves 6*

1 medium sized chicken
1 tsp red chilli powder
2 green chillies
2 tsps vinegar
3 tsps chopped onion
1/2 tsp white pepper (ground)
2 tsps ghee
2 garlic flakes
2 1/2 or 3 cups milk
6 tsps butter
1 cup stock of chicken
4 tsps flour
5 tsps tomato sauce
1 small piece of ginger
1 full boiled egg
2 bay leaves

Boil chicken pieces with garlic flakes, vinegar and 3 cups of water and bay leaf, till they becomes tender. Remove the pieces from the stock. Now fry the flour in butter, with green chillies and onion (finely chopped) and fry till very slightly golden brown. Add milk and stock, cook till mixture is thick but not very thick. Mix salt. If the mixture is thin then mix one tsp cornflour mixed in 1/4 cup of water and cook for a few minutes. At the time of serving add 4 tsps tomato sauce and mix lightly. Arrange boiled egg pieces. Melt 2 tsps ghee, then in it add red chilli powder. Keep it till red in colour and then pour over the chicken. Serve it at lunch or dinner.

GOANESE CHICKEN CURRY   serves 6

1 chicken ¾ kg	2 onions
4 tsps ground dry coriander	6 garlic flakes
	1 tsp red chilli powder
2 tsps long strips of ginger	½ cup ghee
6 green cardamoms	1 tsp poppy seeds
salt to taste	1 tsp curd
2 tsps ground spices	1 tsp dry fenugreek leaves

Cut the chicken into small pieces. Fry ground onion, garlic, and whole cardamoms until light brown. Add red chilli powder, curd, chicken pieces and stir until dry. Add ground poppy seeds, fenugreek, ground spices, coriander, ginger strips and salt and sufficient water and cook on slow fire until tender and gravy is thick. Serve hot at lunch or dinner.

KASHMIRI CHICKEN CURRY   serves 6

1 medium sized chicken	1 big onion
5 garlic flakes	4 small fresh ginger pieces
5 green cardamoms	1 tsp red chilli powder
1½ cups buttermilk or sour milk	½ cup thick cream
	2 medium sized tomatoes
¼ cup cashewnuts	¼ cup peeled and ground almonds
salt to taste	
½ cup ghee	

Chop the onion and then fry in ghee with cardamoms until light brown, then add ginger and garlic water (grind garlic and ginger with ½ cup of water then squeeze out the liquid) and stir for 5 minutes. Now add chicken pieces, small pieces of tomatoes and red chilli and cook for 5 minutes. Add buttermilk, salt, cashewnuts and almonds and enough water and cook over low heat until the chicken is tender. Remove from fire. At the time of serving pour cream over chicken curry and mix lightly. Serve at dinner or lunch.

CHICKEN MASALA CURRY *serves 6*

1 chicken ³/₄ kg
6 slices of fresh ginger (ground)
1 tsp dry coriander
1 tsp poppy seeds
salt to taste
1 tsp red chilli powder
2 tsps curd
2 onions
2 tsps tomato (paste)
8 garlic cloves
1 tsp cuminseeds
5 green cardamoms
½ cup ghee
113 gms tomato
42 gms long strips of ginger

Soak poppy seeds for 15 minutes. Grind ginger, garlic, onion, coriander and cuminseeds and fry until brown, then add a little water and stir. Now add chicken pieces and stir until dry. Add ground poppy seeds, almonds, cardamoms, chopped tomato, salt and red chilli powder and fry till dry. Add long strips of ginger, curd and stir for a few minutes. Now add tomato sauce, 2 cups of hot water and keep on slow fire until tender. Serve hot.

MUGHLAI MAKHANI CHICKEN CURRY *serves 6*

1 medium sized chicken
8 green cardamoms
1 tsp ground ginger
⅛ tsp grated nutmeg
1 tsp red chilli powder
1 cup curd
15 garlic cloves (ground)
1 very small piece of mace
salt to taste

Cut the chicken into small pieces. Mix all the ingredients into a smooth paste and then marinate the chicken pieces in it for 2 hours. Stick on iron skewers and roast in moderate tandoor or on wire rack in oven until dry and tender.

Tomato Gravy
140 gms butter
1 small onion
1 tsp chopped coriander leaves
salt to taste
56 gms almonds
½ kg tomatoes
2 green chillies
2 garlic cloves
½ tsp red chilli powder
2 cloves
1 cinnamon piece (¼")

Chop the tomatoes, garlic, coriander leaves and onion and then cook with cloves, cinnamon and red chilli powder in pan on slow fire until tomatoes are tender. Pass through a sieve. Heat butter, mix tomato pulp, ground almonds, thin slices of green chillies and roasted chicken pieces. Cook for a few minutes. Serve hot at lunch or dinner.

MAKHANI CHICKEN CURRY　　　　　　serves 6

1 small tandoori chicken (see the recipe of tandoori chicken).
2 tsps sugar
$1/2$ level tsp red chilli powder
$1/2$ cup butter
salt to taste
$1/2$ kg tomatoes
1 bay leaf
1 tsp ground ginger
1 small capsicum

Cook chopped tomatoes, ginger and bay leaf till tender. Pass through a sieve. Mix red chilli, powder, salt and sugar and chicken pieces into tomato pulp. Cook till it boils. Add capsicum without seeds, cook for a few minutes, mix butter and sprinkle coriander leaves. Serve with nan.

MURG MUSULAM　　　　　　　　　　serves 6

1 medium sized chicken
2 big cardamoms
4 green cardamoms
3 cloves
2 tbsps ghee
56 gms peeled almonds
salt to taste
$2^{1}/_{2}$ level tsps cornflour
A few drops of kewara flavour
3 medium onions
1 small piece of cinnamon
2 small pieces of ginger
1 bay leaf
2 tsps poppy seeds
$2^{1}/_{2}$ cups milk
$1/4$ cup khoya
few coriander leaves
3 green chillies
1 small piece of coconut

Cook chicken with green cardamoms, cloves, onion, ginger, big cardamoms and 2 cups of water until tender. Soak poppy seeds in water. Grind coconut, peeled almonds and soaked poppy finely. Mix khoya, ground almonds, poppy and coconut into milk and cook for a few mintues. Add cornflour mixed with $1/2$ cup water to milk until a little thick. Add meat with spices, salt, chopped green chillies coriander leaves and kewara flavour and cook for a few minutes. Serve hot at dinner.

NARGASI CHICKEN CURRY serves 6

1½ chicken
2 tsps cloves
5 green cardamoms
½ kg spinach leaves
14 gms ginger
½ tsp saffron
28 gms khoya
salt to taste

½ cup ghee
½ tsp black pepper
14 gms dry coriander powder
1 tsp red chilli powder
8 garlic flakes
113 gms onion
2 eggs

Heat 3 oz ghee and fry the chicken pieces until brown. Remove them from ghee. Fry finely chopped onion and garlic in the same ghee and fry until golden brown. Add coriander powder, salt, red chilli powder, meat with enough water to cover it and cook on slow fire until the chicken is tender. Grind cloves, cardamoms and ginger to a fine paste and add to the meat. Dissolve saffron in a little water and stir it into the meat, fry well for 10 minutes. Remove the meat from the masala and keep aside. In a separate vessel heat remaining ghee (2 oz), fry well washed and chopped spinach leaves with the masala from the meat and khoya and cook on slow fire until the spinach is cooked and dry. Now place the spinach in frying pan, lightly beat the egg and spread it on the spinach. When the egg sets, place the chicken pieces over it and place in a serving dish. Serve it at lunch or dinner.

TANDOORI ROASTED CHICKEN CURRY serves 4

1 chicken ¾ kg
¼ cup ghee
4 big pieces of ginger
1 tsp red chillies
3 pieces of cinnamon
   (1 inch piece)

12 or 15 garlic flakes
½ tsp saffron
1 cup curd
6 green cardamoms
1 piece mace
salt to taste

Grind green cardamoms, cinnamon, mace and garlic finely. Grind ginger separately with 3 tbsps of water and then strain it. Mix above ground and ginger water in curd. Clean and wash the chicken and dry with duster. Prick it with kitchen fork and keep it soaked in curd for two hours.

Leave 8 inches space of iron skewer from the bottom and first put a small round ball of kneaded atta and then pack chicken tightly. Lastly put again a ball of kneaded atta which helps to keep the chicken tightly on the skewer. Grill the chicken in the tandoor and cover it. Fire must be slow. When chicken is tender and all the curd is absorbed then baste it frequently with ghee on strong heat until brown in colour; cover the tandoor. Sprinkle juice of $1/2$ lemon over the chicken. Serve hot at dinner or lunch. (Chicken can be grilled in oven.)

TANDOORI MIXED GRILL   serves 4

$1/2$ kg (chicken pieces, mutton flat pieces, liver, kidney and kapura)
2 level tsps salt
1 tsp red chilli powder

1 tsp ground ginger
water of 20 garlic flakes
4 cardamoms
$1/2$ cup curd
1 tsp peeled and ground papaya juice

Mix all the ingredients, keep it for two hours. Then stick on iron rod and keep it in very moderate tandoor till dry. Then pour ghee over the meat and again keep in tandoor till dry. Now sprinkle 1 tsp spices and lemon juice. (Cook mutton pieces, liver, kidney, kapura and chicken pieces till $3/4$ tender. Cool, mix all the above.)

ROASTED TEETAR   serves 4

3 medium sized teetars
2 tsps ginger
1 tsp red chilli powder
salt to taste
$1 1/2$ kitchen spoon ghee

15 garlic flakes
1 heaped cup curd
$1/2$ tsp cinnamon powder
6 green cardamoms

For Gravy
3 medium sized onions
1 tsp sugar
1 tsp ground spices
1 tsp ginger

3 medium sized tomatoes
5 garlic flakes
250 gms peas
salt to taste

Mix ground cardamoms, cinnamon, red chilli powder, ginger, garlic and salt into curd, then rub on the teetar and keep it for 8 hours or overnight. Cook with 1 or 2 cups of water and ghee till tender and dry. Then fry till nicely browned. Remove the ghee from the fried teetar and in this ghee fry chopped onion till light brown. Add ground garlic, ginger, one cup of water, and salt and cook till dry. Add peeled and chopped tomatoes and sugar and stir till it leaves its ghee. Add boiled peas. Add fried teetar in masala and cook for a few minutes. Garnish with coriander leaves and serve.

BENGALI FISH CURRY   serves 8

3/4 kg rohu fish
1/2 tsp turmeric
20 garlic flakes
2 tsps ground spices
1 tsp red chilli powder
3/4 cup ghee

170 gms onion
225 gms tomatoes
6 small pieces of ginger
1 tsp ground amchoor
salt to taste

Fry ground garlic and onion in shallow pan until brown. Add I cup of water, turmeric, ground ginger, red chilli powder, salt, chopped tomatoes and stir until dry. Add 3 cups of water and boil the gravy and then add medium pieces of fish. Keep the pan uncovered and cook on very slow fire until tender and gravy is thick. Mix dry mango and ground spices lightly. Don't stir but only shake the pan occasionally to prevent the fish sticking to the pan. Serve hot at lunch or dinner with boiled rice.

FISH KEEMA CURRY   serves 6

1/2 kg rohu fish
2 big onions
6 cloves
2-inch piece of ginger
a few coriander leaves
1/2 tsp turmeric
140 gms ghee
salt to taste

15 garlic flakes
2 bay leaves
6 green cardamoms
2 1/2 tsps ground dry
  coriander
225 gms curd
1 tsp red chilli powder

Clean the fish and cut into large pieces, cook in vessel or pan with 2 cups of water, bay leaves and cardamoms on very slow fire until tender. Strain the stock through a fine sieve and keep aside. Remove the bones from the fish and then mash it coarsely. Grind onion, garlic, ginger with chilli powder and turmeric to a fine paste and mix into curd with ground spices and dry coriander. Heat ghee and fry mashed fish for a few minutes and then stir in it ground masala mixed in curd until golden brown. Add the stock obtained from boiling fish and cook till stock evaporates. Garnish with coriander leaves. Serve hot at lunch or dinner.

KASHMIRI FISH CURRY serves 6

750 gms sagara fish
2 big onions
2 tbsps flour
$1/2$ tsp turmeric
1 tsp red chilli powder
140 gms ghee
225 gms tomatoes

2 tsps lemon juice
15 garlic flakes
$1/2$ cup finely ground blanced almonds
2 tsps ground spices
1 tsp coriander leaves
$1/2$ tsp black pepper

Clean and wash fish. Dry it with a cloth and then cut into big pieces. Rub salt and lemon juice and then keep aside. Fry ground onion and garlic until brown, add turmeric, one cup of water and salt, red chilli powder and peeled and chopped tomatoes and stir until it leaves the ghee. Add two cups of water and ground almonds and cook until gravy is thick. Remove from fire. Dust the fish with flour and fry till golden brown and then put in gravy, spinkle black pepper and chopped coriander leaves on it. Serve hot at dinner or lunch.

MUGHLAI FISH CURRY serves 6

$1/2$ kg pomfret fish
1 tsp ground fresh ginger
2 tsps chopped coriander leaves
$1/4$ tsp ground cinnamon
3 ground cloves
$1/2$ coconut

2 big onions
8 garlic flakes
2 tsps ground cuminseeds
170 gms ghee
1 big tomato
$1/2$ tsp turmeric

8 peppercorns
4 green cardamons
salt to taste
1 tsp red chilli powder

Clean and wash the fish. Cut into big pieces. Grind peppercorns, red chilli powder, salt, turmeric and ground spices to a smooth paste with a little water. Heat ghee, fry chopped onion and garlic with cardamoms until golden brown. Add ground spices paste and ground ginger and one cup of water. Stir until onion is tender, mix chopped and peeled tomatoes and stir until thick. Add $1^1/_2$ cups of thin coconut juice or milk and fried fish, cook till gravy is thick. Remove from fire and sprinkle chopped coriander leaves on it and serve hot lunch or dinner.

FISH KOFTA CURRY *serves 6*

$3/_4$ kg rohu fish
226 gms tomatoes
15 garlic flakes
3 tsps ground spices
1 tsp chopped coriander leaves
2 big onions
1 tsp ground ginger
1 tsp red chilli powder
salt to taste
1 egg yolk
$1/_2$ cup ghee

Clean and wash the fish. Boil in salted water until tender. Cool, remove the bones and skin and mash it, mix one tsp ground spices and salt to taste and yolk of egg in it. Make 16 round balls and dust with flour and fry until light brown and then keep the koftas aside. Fry ground onion and garlic until brown, add one cup of water, salt, red chilli powder, spices, ginger, chopped and peeled tomatoes and stir until dry. Add $2^1/_2$ cups of water and cook till gravy is thick and then gently add the fish balls and cook on slow fire for 5 minutes in the pan uncovered. Don't stir the curry but shake the vessel or pan occasionally. Sprinkle chopped coriander leaves on it. Serve hot at dinner or lunch.

PLUM FISH KOFTA CURRY

See recipe of Fish Kofta Curry.
Same and same method of fish kofta curry. But here fill dry plums in each kofta, dust it with flour and dry in deep and

hot ghee till golden brown (soak plums in water for 15 minutes before filling in koftas).

STUFFED FISH TOMATO CURRY   serves 8

250 grams fish $1/4$ tsp black pepper
   (sole or singhara)   2 bread slices
10 tomatoes (firm)   2 green chillies
1 tsp ground cuminseeds   salt to taste
few coriander leaves

Scoop out the pulp from tomatoes. Steam the fish, remove bones and skin, mash it. Mix soaked and squeezed bread slices, chopped green chillies, coriander leaves, salt, pepper and cumin. Fill it in the tomatoes. Cook in the gravy till a little tender. (Gravy is the same as for Stuffed Keema Tomato Curry.)

FISH VINDALOO CURRY   serves 8

$1/2$ kg fish (without $1/2$ tsp red chilli powder
   bones and skin) $1/2$ cup vinegar
1 tsp salt   flour for dusting
ghee for shallow drying   1 tsp ground cumin

Cut the cleaned fish into medium pieces. Make a paste of vinegar, red chilli powder, salt and cumin powder and rub over the fish pieces. Keep aside for 10 minutes. Dust with flour and fry in hot ghee till golden brown. Remove from ghee and keep them aside.

Gravy

1 cup grated onion   2 tsp chopped ginger
8 garlic flakes   4 medium sized tomatoes
1 tsp red chilli powder   2 tsps ground cumin
1 tsp ground   3 cloves
   coriander seeds   2 tsps ground mustard seeds
$1/4$ cup vinegar   a few coriander leaves
2 tsps ground poppy seeds   1 cup melted ghee
$1/2$ tsp black pepper   salt to taste

Fry grated onion till light golden brown. Add one cup water, ground garlic and ginger. Cook till dry. Add peeled and chopped tomatoes and all the ground spices, salt and stir till dry. Add 3 cups of water, cook till about $1\frac{1}{2}$ cups of water is left. Add fish and vinegar, cook for a few minutes. Garnish with coriander leaves. Serve it at lunch or dinner.

AFGHANI MUTTON CURRY   serves 6

$\frac{1}{2}$ kg mutton
2 tsps ground ginger
1 cup curd or $1\frac{1}{2}$ cups of sour milk
$\frac{1}{2}$ tsp ground cinnamon
4 cloves
$1\frac{1}{2}$ tbsps ghee
$\frac{1}{4}$ tsp orange colour

16 garlic flakes
1 tsp red chilli powder
6 green cardamoms
1 small piece of mace
$\frac{1}{4}$ tsp grated nutmeg
113 gms peas (boiled in salted water)
a few chopped coriander leaves

Put meat, ground garlic, ginger, ghee, 2 cups of water and salt in a vessel and cook till dry and almost tender. Now add all the ground spices, curd, red chilli powder and colour. Fry till dry. Put the mixture in dish, then garnish with boiled peas and coriander leaves.

DALWALA MEAT   serves 6

$\frac{3}{4}$ kg mutton
4 cloves
3 tsps white cuminseeds
2 cinnamons
1 tsp red chilli powder
2 tsps ground fresh ginger
$\frac{3}{4}$ tsp turmeric
6 tsps dry coriander

10 flakes of garlic
170 gms urad dal (black gram)
3 medium sized onions
2 cardamoms
1 big tomato
salt to taste
2 tsps fresh coriander leaves

Soak dal for 15 minutes. Boil water with $\frac{1}{2}$ tsp salt and $\frac{1}{4}$ tsp turmeric and then add dal and cook until tender. Fry chopped onions with cloves, cinnamon and cardamoms until light brown. Add ground garlic and ginger, red chilli powder and tomato and stir for a few minutes. Add meat, ground cuminseeds and dry coriander and stir until water of meat is absorbed. Add dal and coriander leaves and cook for a few minutes. Serve hot at lunch or dinner.

DAHIWALA MEAT serves 6

3/4 kg mutton
2 tsps ground ginger
6 green cardamoms
1 bay leaf
1 cup chopped onion
340 gms curd
170 gms tomatoes
2 pieces of cinnamon

15 garlic flakes
4 cloves
2 big cardamoms
2 tbsps ghee
salt to taste
1 tsp red chillies
2 tsps white cumin powder

Fry chopped onion with cinnamon, cloves, cardamoms, green cardamoms, bay leaf, till golden brown. Add a cup of water, ground garlic and ginger and stir well till dry. Now add meat, salt, red chilli powder, ground white cuminseeds and water and cook it till half tender. Add curd and peeled and chopped tomatoes and cook on slow fire till tender. Garnish with coriander and serve at lunch or dinner.

GOANESE MUTTON CURRY serves 6

3/4 kg mutton
5 green cardamoms
2 tsps khus khus
   (poppy seeds)
1 tsp chopped ginger
fresh coconut or
   dry coconut
4 medium sized onions
juice of 1/2 lemon

1 small piece of cinnamon
2 tsps cumin or white jeera
12 garlic flakes
5 cloves
3 tsps red chilli powder
4 cups of water
salt to taste
1/2 cup ghee
2 green chillies

Fry chopped onion until light brown. Add garlic, ginger and one cup of water and cook until onion is tender. Grind cinnamon, cardamom khus khus, cloves, white zeera and ground coconut (remove the brown part of the coconut) with a little water. Add masala and meat and fry until dry. Add hot water and cook on medium fire until tender, then add long strips of green chillies. Mix lime juice 10 minutes before serving. Serve hot at lunch or dinner with chapatti.

KIDNEY KORMA   serves 6

10 kidneys
6 garlic flakes
1 level tsp red chilli powder
4 green cardamoms
2 tsps white jeera
2 tsps lemon juice
few coriander leaves
1 tsp ground poppy seeds
$1/2$ tsp turmeric (haldi)
$1/2$ cup chopped onions
1 tsp ginger
5 peeled almonds
$1/2$ tsp ground cinnamon
6 ground cloves
2 tsps dry coriander
salt to taste
2 tsps tomato ketchup
1 tbsp ghee

Cut the kidney into four pieces and wash them. Fry chopped onions till light brown, add ground garlic, ginger and a cup of water. Cook till dry, then add all the ground spicies, turmeric, red chilli powder, almond and poppy seeds, one cup of water, kidney and salt and cook on slow fire till a little dry and then fry them well. Put them on a serving dish, garnish with coriander and long strips of green chillies.

IRANI MUTTON CURRY   serves 6

$1/2$ kg mutton
4 cloves
2 cinnamon pieces
2 or 3 tbsps curd
6 tsps dry coriander
salt to taste
A few coriander leaves
113 gms onion
10 garlic flakes
1 tsp red chilli powder
7 big cardamoms
2 tomatoes
3 tsps white cuminseeds
long and thin strips of ginger
$1/2$ cup ghee

Grind coriander, white cuminseeds finely. Fry chopped onion with cloves, cinnamon and cardamoms, until brown, then add ground garlic, ground coriander, cuminseeds, chopped tomatoes, curd, meat, salt, red chilli powder and fry until water of meat is absorbed. Add 4 cups of water and long strips of ginger and cook on slow fire until meat is tender and a little dry. Garnish with coriander leaves. Serve hot.

MUTTON DO PIAZA   serves 6

- ½ kg meat
- 225 gms onion
- 2 small pieces of fresh ginger
- 113 gms tomatoes
- 2 tsps white cuminseeds
- 4 whole red chillies
- ½ inch piece of cinnamon
- 170 gms ghee
- 10 flakes of garlic
- curd
- 1 tsp red chilli
- 3 cloves
- 6 black peppercorns
- 6 green cardamoms
- 1 big cardamom
- 1 bay leaf
- salt to taste

Cut thin and round slices of onion, chop garlic and cut long and thin slices of ginger. Fry 6 gms onion until golden brown, then add meat, salt, red chilli powder, peeled and chopped tomatoes, ginger and garlic and fry till meat is dry. Add curd, 3 cups of water, 2 gms onion slices, black pepper, whole chillies, bay leaf, cinnamon, white cuminseeds, cloves and cardamoms and cook on slow fire until meat is tender. Serve hot at lunch or dinner.

MUTTON MAGAJ CURRY   serves 6

- ½ kg mutton
- 2 tsp ground ginger
- 4 whole dry red chillies
- 1 tsp red chilli powder
- 4 tsps dry coriander
- 1 tsp black cumin
- ¼ cup vinegar
- 56 gms magaj (melon seeds)
- 1 tsp fenugreek leaves
- 170 gms ghee
- 10 garlic flakes
- 6 green cardamoms
- 1 tsp chopped onions
- 4 green chillies strips without seeds
- 1 cup curd
- 2 tsps poppy seeds
- 56 gms coconut
- coriander leaves

Grind black cumin and green cardamoms, dry coriander, poppy seeds and coconut. Soak meat in vinegar. Fry chopped onion till golden brown. Add ground garlic and ginger and one cup of water and stir till dry. Add red chilli powder, fenugreek leaves, ground spices, and mutton and stir till dry. Add 3 cups of water and cook on slow fire till tender. Sprinkle fried magaj, chopped coriander leaves and long strips of green chillies.

MULTANI MEAT CURRY serves 8

$3/4$ kg meat
3 tsps ground ginger
2 medium sized tomatoes
few coriander leaves
salt to taste
2 tsps lemon juice
2 tsps ground spices

1 cup chopped onions
12 garlic flakes (thin)
9 tsps dry coriander
$1^1/2$ tsps red chilli powder
2 tsps tomato ketchup
5 tsps cuminseeds
170 gms ghee

Fry the chopped onions till golden brown. Add ground ginger and garlic and one cup of water and cook till dry. Add ground wet coriander, cumin, salt, $3/4$ tsp of red chilli powder, meat and peeled and chopped tomatoes and cook till dry. Add 3 or 4 cups of water till the meat is tender and a little dry. At the time of serving mix tomato ketchup and lemon juice. Melt 3 tsp ghee, remove from fire and mix $1/2$ tsp of red chilli powder in it. Put the meat in a dish and on top of it pour ghee of red chillies and garnish with coriander leaves.

MINCED MEAT WITH PANEER CURRY serves 6

$1/2$ kg minced meat thick
2 tsps ginger
$1^1/2$ tsps kasoori methi
 or fenugreek leaves
25 gms paneer
4 tsps melon seeds
1 tsp red chilli powder
$1^1/2$ tsps cuminseeds
 (ground)
1 bay leaf

$3/4$ cup chopped onion
10 garlic flakes
225 gms peas
25 gms tomatoes
5 green cardamoms
few coriander leaves
$1^1/2$ tsps ground spices
1 small capsicum
$1^1/2$ tsps ghee
salt to taste

Fry the chopped onions with bay leaf, green cardamoms till nicely brown. Then add ground garlic, ginger and $1^1/2$ cups of water and cook till water is evaporated. Add peas and minced meat, half of red chilli powder, ground spices, white cumin, salt to taste and cook till the water is evaporated. Add peeled and chopped tomatoes, $1^1/2$ or 2 cups of water and cook till minced meat is tender. Add fried paneer and cook till water is evaporated. Then add chopped capsicum and cook for a few minutes. In 4 tsps ghee (heated), put red chilli powder and melon seeds and then pour the ghee over the dish and garnish with coriander leaves.

MUTTON VINDALOO CURRY

serves 6

1/2 kg mutton
3 tsps white cuminseeds
2 tsps dry fenugreek leaves
2 medium onions
6 small pieces of fresh ginger
170 gms ghee

6 tsps dry coriander
1/2 tsp peppercorns
6 tsps vinegar
2 level tsps mustard seeds
10 garlic flakes
2 tsps red chilli powder
salt to taste

Grind finely dry coriander, cuminseeds, pepper corns, mustard seeds and dry fenugreek leaves, chop onion and fry in ghee until light brown. Add ground garlic and ginger and fry for a few minutes. Add ground spices, mutton pieces, red chilli powder, salt and vinegar and fry the meat until dry. Pour enough water and cover the vessel tightly and put some weight on the lid of the vessel. Heat on slow fire until meat is tender and water is absorbed and it leaves its ghee. Serve hot.

STUFFED CAULIFLOWER WITH MINCED MEAT

serves 6

1 medium size cauliflower
1 green chilli
3 medium size tomatoes
2 tsps ground ginger
2 green cardamoms
2 tsps white cuminseeds ground
2 tsps ground ginger for cauliflower

250 gms minced meat
few coriander leaves
1 bay leaf
6 thick garlic flakes
1 tsp red chilli powder
1 tsp ground spices
2 tsps fenugreek leaves
3/4 cup grated onion
1 kitchen tsp ghee

Soak the cauliflower in enough water with 2 tsps salt for about 35 minutes. Then put it on the strainer so that water may trickle down. Rub 2 tsp ground ginger water over it. Then fry it golden brown in shallow pan from all the sides.

Remove from the ghee. Fry the grated onion till light brown. Add ground garlic, ginger, bay leaf and 1 cup of water. Cook till the water is evaporated. Add peeled and chopped tomatoes, ground spices, ground white cuminseeds, salt, red chilli powder, fenugreek leaves, green cardamoms and minced meat and cook till dry. Add 3 cups of water and cook till the keema is tender. Cook the cauliflower in the minced meat till tender and gravy becomes thick. At the time of serving put it in the dish and sprinkle with coriander leaves and chopped green chillies.

SHAHI KORMA   serves 6

750 gms meat   1½ onions
7 garlic flakes   12 ginger slices
1 tsp chilli powder   2 tsps white cuminseeds
1 tsp dry coriander   140 gms ghee
55 gms almonds   1½ tsps poppy seeds
7 cardamoms   56 gms khoya
2 cups milk   salt to taste

Grind finely onion, garlic, ginger, cuminseeds and dry coriander and fry in ghee until golden brown. Add red chilli powder, meat and fry until dry. Add milk and cook on very slow fire until dry. Grind finely 1 oz peeled almonds, green cardamons and poppy seeds and then mix into meat. Add salt and water and cook till tender. Add 1 oz peeled almonds and khoya and cook for few minutes. Serve hot at lunch or dinner.

MUTTON ROLLS WITH TOMATO SAUCE   serves 6

250 gms minced meat   2 chopped green chillies
3 tsps chopped onion   1 tsp heaped flour
3 eggs   2 tsps white cuminseeds
½ tsp salt

Cook the minced meat with one cup of water till it becomes dry. Fry the flour, green chillies and onion in one tsp ghee till light brown. Add cooked minced meat, salt and coriander leaves. Cook for one or two minutes. Remove from fire and cool. Beat egg with ¼ tsp salt for 1 or 2 minutes. Make very thin omelettes in greased frying pan. Fill the minced meat mixture and then roll into the omelettes and again fry them in shallow ghee. Make tomato sauce and spread it around the omelette rolls in an oval shaped dish, add coriander leaves for garnishing.

Sauce

tomatoes	1 bay leaf
salt to taste	1 or 2 tsps sugar
$1/2$ level tsp red chilli powder	

Cut the tomatoes into small pieces, then cook with all the ingredients till tender. Pass it through a sieve, and cook. If the sauce is thin then mix 1 tsp cornflour mixed in $1/4$ cup of water. Mix it in tomato sauce and cook. If the colour is not good mix 2 drops orange colour and one drop red colour.

ROASTED MUTTON LEG   serves 6

1 kg mutton leg	6 green cardamoms
$1/4$ tsp ground cinnamon	12 garlic flakes
2 tsps ginger	1 tsp level red chilli powder
6 or 8 tsps curd	ghee for shallow frying
$1/4$ tsp dry, sweet orange colour	$1 1/2$ tsps salt
	1 lemon
1 onion slices	1 tomato

Cook the mutton leg with ground garlic, ground, ginger, and 1 tsp salt, and water till it becomes tender and dry. (It depends on the meat.) In a pressure cooker put $2 1/2$ cups of water. Make a paste of curd, red chilli powder, ground cinnamons, ground cardamoms, $1/2$ tsp salt and orange colour. In it soak the mutton leg, for at least 1 hour. Then fry it in shallow ghee (very little ghee) on slow fire till it becomes dry. Now serve it with tomato and onion slices and mint chutney.

ROGAN JOSH   serves 8

$3/4$ kg meat	4 onions
20 garlic flakes	10 fresh ginger slices
2 tsps white cuminseed	2 tsps dry coriander

4 cloves
2 big cardamoms
225 gms tomatoes
salt to taste
$1^1/_2$ tsps red chilli powder
2 big pieces of cinnamon
3 or 4 tbsps ghee

Fry chopped onion, garlic, big cardamoms and cinnamon until light brown. Add one cup of water, salt, and ground ginger and stir until onion is tender, add meat, cook till it absorbs its water. Add peeled and chopped tomatoes ground spices and stir until dry. Add water and cook on slow fire until meat is tender and gravy is thick. Put tomatoes in hot water for a few minutes and then peel them. Add the tomato puree to the rogan josh.

STUFFED KEEMA TOMATO CURRY serves 8

Stuffing
250 gms minced meat
3 green chillies
$1/_4$ tsp black pepper
$1/_4$ kitchen tsp ghee
4 garlic flakes
salt to taste
10 tomatoes (medium size)
8 small onion
$1^1/_2$ tsps ground cumin
a few coriander leaves
1 tsp ginger

Fry chopped onion till light brown. Add ground garlic, ginger and $1/_2$ cup of water and cook till dry. Now add all the ingredients of stuffing except coriander and tomatoes and cook with one cup of water till tender and dry. Scoop out the pulp from tomatoes. Cool the stuffing, mix coriander and fill into the tomatoes.

Gravy
1 cup onion (grated)
2 tsp ginger
$1^1/_2$ level tsps red chilli powder
2 tsps ground spices
1 kitchen tbsp ghee
7 garlic flakes
pulp of 10 tomatoes
1 tsp white cumin
1 tsp sugar
salt to taste

Fry onion till light brown. Then add ground garlic and ginger and a cup of water and cook till dry. Add all the ingredients, 3 cups of water and cook till gravy is a little thick. Cook stuffed tomatoes in it for five minutes till a little tender, garnish with coriander and serve.

CREAM KOFTA CURRY   serves 8

Kofta

$1/2$ kg minced meat	56 gms chana dal
3 cloves	2 cups water
1 cinnamon ($1/4$")	1 big cardamom
4 green cardamoms	$1/2$ tsp dry coriander
1 tsp white pepper	1 tsp cuminseed
salt to taste	5 almonds (blanched)
2 eggs	breadcrumbs
56 gms khoya	

Cook all the above with enough water except khoya, breadcrumbs and eggs until tender and dry, cool and then grind finely. Mix in it 1 or 2 egg yolks. Make 12 flat round balls and in each fill khoya mixed with chopped almonds. Coat with breatcrumbs and then dip in unbeaten egg whites and fry until very light brown in colour.

Gravy

3 cups milk	2 tsps poppy seeds
blanched almonds	55 gms khoya
salt to taste	3 level tsps cornflour
2 drops of kewara flavour	2 green chillies
a few coriander leaves	a small piece of fresh coconut

Soak poppy seeds in a little water for a few minutes. Grind coconut, blanched almonds and soaked poppy seeds finely. Mix khoya and ground ingredients in milk and cook for a few minutes and then add cornflour mixed with a little water until a little thick. Add fried koftas, chopped green chillies, coriander leaves, white pepper, salt and two drops of kewara flavour and cook a for few minutes. Serve hot at lunch or dinner.

NARGASI KOFTA CURRY   serves 6

Kofta

340 gms minced meat	6 boiled eggs
85 gms chana dal	1 small piece of cinnamon
2 cardamoms	1 beaten egg
3 cloves	2 tsps coriander leaves

10 peppercorns
salt to taste
1 level tsp chilli powder
ghee for frying

Cook 8 oz minced meat, chana dal, cinnamon, cardamom, cloves, peppercorns, chilli powder and salt until tender. Cool and grind finely with coriander leaves and 4 oz uncoked minced meat and then mix in it beaten egg. Divide the mixture into 6 or 7 portions and then in it fill boiled eggs and make into egg shapes. Deep fry in ghee until golden brown.

Gravy

225 gms onions
28 gms ginger
2 tsps chopped chopped coriander leaves
1 tsp red chilli powder
salt to taste
56 gms khoya
2 tsps ground white cuminseeds
10 garlic flakes
225 gms tomatoes
6 green cardamoms (ground)
4 tbsps ghee
4 tsps ground spices
1 tsp chopped coriander leaves

Fry chopped onion and garlic until light brown. Add salt and one cup of water and cook till onion is tender. Add peeled and chopped tomatoes, ground ginger, red chilli powder, ground spices, white cuminseeds, green cardamoms and coriander leaves and stir until it becomes a thick gravy. Add khoya and stir for a few minutes. Add 3 cups water and cook till $1^1/_2$ cup water is left. Remove from fire. Cut koftas lengthwise, arrange on gravy and sprinkle coriander leaves on them. Serve hot at lunch or dinner.

PUNJABI KOFTA CURRY   serves 6

Koftas

$1/_2$ kg minced meat
1 tsp chopped coriander leaves
2 green chillies chopped
1 tsp chopped ginger
1 tsp ground spices
$1/_2$ tsp black pepper
salt to taste

Mix all the above into minced meat. Make 12 round balls the size of a large walnut, with wet hand. Boil the water with a little salt and in it put koftas. Cook in an uncovered pan until firm. Remove from the water and keep it aside.

Gravy

3 big onions
1 tsp ground ginger
6 green cardamoms
1 tsp ground cuminseeds
2 tsps chopped
   coriander leaves
3 big tomatoes
15 garlic flakes
2 tsps ground spices
1 tsp red chilli powder
170 gms ghee

Fry ground onion, garlic and whole cardamoms until golden brown. Add one cup of water, chopped and peeled tomatoes, ground ginger, red chilli powder and all the ground spices and stir until thick. Fry boiled koftas in thick gravy for a few minutes. Add sufficient water in which koftas have boiled, and cook until gravy is thick. Sprinkle chopped coriander. Serve hot at lunch or dinner.

PLUM KOFTA CURRY   serves 8

Kofta

$1/2$ kg minced meat
3 small pieces of ginger
$1 1/2$ tsps salt
113 gms dry plums
2 tsps white cuminseed
1 green chilli
5 green cardamoms
a few coriander leaves
1 tsp ground spices

Soak plums in water for 15 minutes. Grind green chilli, ginger, white cuminseeds, green cardamoms and coriander leaves and mix into the minced meat. Add salt and spices and mix well. Make 20 round balls a size bigger than walnuts and in each fill plums.

Gravy

3 onions
14 gms ginger
170 gms tomatoes
1 tsp red chilli powder
4 green cardamons
15 flakes of garlic
6 tbsps ghee
salt to taste
2 tsps ground spices
a few coriander leaves

Grind onions and fry it until light brown. Add ground ginger, and garlic, chopped tomatoes, red chilli powder, ground green cardamoms, ground spices and salt. Fry till dry. Add 8 cups of water and cook gravy for 10 minutes. Add koftas and cook (in uncovered pan) till tender and gravy is a little thick. Remove from fire and serve hot at lunch or dinner.

MUTTON AND EGG KOFTA CURRY   serves 6

Kofta
340 gms minced meat
2 tsps chopped ginger (chopped finely)
1 big piece of cinnamon (1")
2 tsps ground white jeera
few coriander leaves
ghee for frying
2 green chillies (chopped)
1 egg
3 cloves
2 big cardamoms
1 bay leaf
salt to taste
$1/4$ cup milk
$1^1/_2$ cup water for minced meat

Cook the minced meat with all the spices, ginger, green chillies and $1^1/_2$ cup of water till it becomes tender and dry. Cool, mix salt and coriander leaves. Grind finely (remove the cinnamon and cloves and peel of big cardamoms). Mix $1/4$ cup of milk and then mix 1 yolk of egg (11 koftas).

Filling
2 full boiled eggs
salt to taste
few coriander leaves
1 green chilli (finely chopped)
$1/2$ tsp ground spices

Grate the boiled eggs. Melt 1 tsp ghee, in it add grated eggs, green chillies, ground spices, coriander leaves and salt to taste. Then cook for 1 or 2 minutes. Make round balls and then fill in the round koftas. Then dip into the unbeaten white of egg, deep fry in ghee till golden brown. Remove from the ghee.

Gravy
1 heaped cup of chopped onion
6 thick garlic flakes
1 tsp ground spices
3 big peeled and chopped tomatoes
few coriander leaves
2 green cardamoms
2 tsps ground spices
1 tsp red chilli powder
2 tsp ground white jeera
1 kitchen tsp ghee
2 bay leaves
salt to taste

Fry the chopped onion in ghee till golden brown, add ground ginger, garlic and 1 cup of water, and cook till the water is evaporated. Add ground spices, ground white jeera, salt, red chilli powder, green cardamoms, peeled and chopped tomatoes and cook till the ghee is separate. Add $2^1/_2$ cups of water and cook till the gravy becomes thick and $^3/_4$ cup of water is left. Put the koftas in serving dish and pour the boiling gravy over it. Then garnish with coriander leaves and serve.

BHUNI KALEJI (Fried Liver)   serves 4

225 gms liver   6 tsps vinegar
4 green chillies   170 gms chopped onions
$^1/_4$ tsp peppercorn   1 tsp cuminseed powder salt
to taste $^1/_4$ cup ghee

Mix all the together with small liver pieces, then fry in ghee till golden. Serve with chappati. (At the time of frying liver wash it 3 to 4 times.)

KABABS

EGG KABABS　　　　　　　　　　　　　*serves 8*

6 hard boiled eggs
1 egg
3/4 cup chopped
　　cooked ham
1 tsp chopped coriander
　　leaves
ghee to fry
4 tsps flour
pinch of nutmeg

1 tsp grated Amul or
　　craft cheese
salt to taste
1/4 tsp white pepper
1 green chilli (chopped)
1 cup dry breadcrumbs
3/4 cup milk
3 tsps butter

Chop finely boiled eggs and ham. Melt butter and in it fry flour until golden in colour, add milk, 1/4 tsp salt, pinch of nutmeg and stir until thick and clears the sides of the pan. Remove from fire, mix chopped boiled eggs, ham, grated cheese, salt, pepper, chopped green chilli and coriander leaves. Chill and then shape into kababs. Dust with flour, dip into beaten egg and roll in breadcrumbs. Fry in hot ghee until golden brown, drain on paper and serve with tomato ketchup at lunch or dinner.

BRAIN KABABS　　　　　　　　　　　　*serves 6*

3 sheep's brains
1 small onion
1 tsp chopped coriander
　　leaves
1 tsp finely chopped ginger
4 tsps vinegar
salt to taste
ghee for shallow frying

3 green chillies
2 slices of bread
1/2 tsp black pepper
1 tsp ground spices
1 tsp ground cuminseed
1 egg
dry breadcrumbs for coating

Wash the brains properly and soak in salted water for 35 minutes. Boil 4 cups of water with vinegar and in it cook brains until firm. Drain and keep aside. Chop onion and green chillies finely. Mix all the chopped, salt, black pepper, ground spices, $1/2$ beaten egg and soaked slices of bread into chopped brains. Make 6 oval shaped balls, dust with flour and then dip in $1/2$ beaten egg and roll up into bread crumbs. Fry in shallow ghee until nicely browned. Put in dish, sprinkle with mint leaves and serve hot at breakfast or tea.

BREAD KABABS WITH FRIED VEGETABLES serves 8

8 bread slices
$1/4$ tsp ground nutmeg
salt to taste
ghee for frying
rind of 1 lemon
$1/4$ tsp ground spices
$1/2$ cup milk
$1/2$ tsp white pepper
2 tsps chopped green coriander leaves
1 egg
1 or $1 1/2$ cup dry breadcrumbs

Cut slices of bread into rectangular shape and $3/4$" thick. Put milk on the plate and dip slices into it. Mix the green coriander leaves, ground spices, lemon rind, salt, pepper, and nutmeg together. Beat egg lightly with $1/4$ cup water, dip the slices into it and then roll into the breadcrumbs and fry in hot ghee in a frying pan till golden brown. Drain on paper, serve hot at tea.

COCKTAIL FISH KABABS serves 8

340 gms fish
3 cups water
4 small pieces of fresh ginger
$1 1/2$ tsps white cuminseeds
ghee for frying
1 inch piece of cinnamon
2 tsps chopped coriander leaves
85 gms chana dal
1 small onion
2 cloves
2 green chillies
1 or 2 egg yolks
$1/4$ tsp red chilli powder
salt to taste
6 garlic flakes

Wash and soak chana dal for 15 minutes. Cook with cloves, cinnamon, cuminseeds and garlic until $3/4$ tender. Drain and keep its water for boiling the fish. Boil fish in chana dal water until tender and water is absorbed. Cool, remove the bones and skin and then grind with chana dal. Grind onion, green chilli, ginger and coriander leaves finely and mix into ground mixture of fish and dal. Mix egg yolks and then form small round balls. Deep fry in ghee until nicely brown in colour. Drain on paper, insert toothpick in each kabab and serve hot at cocktail party.

FISH CAKES OR KABABS   serves 6

28 gms cleaned fish
3 green chillies
170 gms boiled potatoes
3 tsps flour
1 tsp chopped coriander leaves
ghee for deep frying

1 onion
$1\frac{1}{2}$ tsps salt
$\frac{3}{4}$ tsp black pepper
1 or 2 eggs
dry breadcrumbs for coating

Boil fish in salted water until tender. Cool and remove the bones and skin and then mash it. Chop onion and green chilli and then fry in one tbsp ghee until light brown. Add flour and coriander leaves and stir for one minute. Mix in it mashed boiled potato, mashed fish, one tsp salt, pepper and cook until it leaves the sides and bottom of the pan clear. Make 5 or 6 shapes of round and flat balls. Beat eggs with 4 tsps flour, 4 tsps water and $\frac{1}{4}$ tsp salt. Dip the fish cakes in it and then roll them in dry breadcrumbs. Deep dry in ghee until nicely browned. Drain on paper. Serve hot with tomato ketchup at lunch or dinner with potato wafers.

FISH ROLL

See the recipe for Fish Cake.
Follow the same method as for Fish Cake. Here shape into rolls.

FISH SEEKH KABABS   serves 6

$\frac{1}{2}$ kg fish
1 egg yolk
1 tsp ground ginger

$1\frac{1}{2}$ tsps ground white cuminseeds
1 tsp ground dry coriander

2 tsps finely chopped onion
salt to taste
3 green chillies
$1/2$ tsp black pepper
ghee for shallow frying

Clean and wash the fish. Boil in salted water until tender. Cool, remove the bones and skin and mash it coarsely. Mix in it ground spices, chopped onion, green chillies, salt, black pepper and yolk of egg and pack it on iron skewers tightly with hand. Make 8 seekh kababs, grill over charcoal fire or grill in oven on wire rack, baste them frequently until golden brown. Brush with ghee to give the glaze and put on low heat for two minutes. Serve hot at lunch or dinner or tea with mint chutney.

FISH KABABS

See the recipe for Seekh Kababs.
Folllow the same method as for Seekh Kababs but make 6 oval shaped balls. Dip into one beaten egg and roll in breadcrumbs. Deep fry in ghee until brown. Serve with tamarind mint chutney. Serve hot at breakfast or tea.

FISH CREAM PEARS   *serves 6*

fish (sole)
3 tsps chopped coriander leaves
28 gms butter
2 tsps salt
$1/4$ tsp black pepper
$1/2$ cup milk
2 eggs
1 tsp chopped onion
25 gms chopped ginger
breadcrumbs for coating
10 tsp flour
2 green chillies
$1/4$ cup cream for filling
$1/2$ cup cream
ghee to fry

Steam the fish, remove bones and skin and mash it coarsely. Fry onion, green chillies, coriander leaves and ginger in butter for a few minutes. Add flour mixed with salt and black pepper and stir until golden in colour. Add milk and cream and stir until thick. Add mashed fish and cook for a few minutes. Remove from fire, and chill. Make ten pears of chilled fish, and in it fill 2 oz whipped cream. Dust with a little flour. Dip in the beaten eggs and roll in breadcrumbs twice. Fry in hot ghee until brown and drain on paper. Decorate with fresh mint leaves and serve hot at dinner party.

COCKTAIL SHAMI KABABS   serves 8

225 gms minced meat
1 medium sized chopped onion
$1/2$ tsp red chillies
3 cloves
6 garlic flakes
2 green chillies
green coriander leaves
3 cardamoms
85 gms chana dal
4 small pieces of fresh ginger
2 egg yolks
$1 1/2$ tsps white cuminseeds
salt to taste
ghee for deep frying
1 small pieces of cinnamon

Cook minced meat and chana dal with onion, ginger, cloves, cuminseed, green chillies, coriander leaves, cinnamon, red chilies, cardamoms, garlic and sufficient water. When tender and water is absorbed remove from fire, mix salt and cool. Grind finely. Mix egg yolks and then form small round shaped balls and deep fry in ghee. Drain on paper. Insert wooden pick in each kabab. Serve hot at cocktail parties with curd chutney.

BARRAH KABABS   serves 6

$3/4$ kg mutton without bones of young lamb
280 gms curd
14 gms fresh ginger
8 green cardamoms
6 tsps papaya juice
20 garlic flakes
56 gms ghee
2 level tsps chilli powder
$1/4$ tsp cinnamon powder
salt to taste
pinch of nutmeg

Wash the meat pieces and cook till $3/4$ tender. Grind ginger and garlic finely. Mix ground garlic and ginger, cinnamon powder, ground cardamoms, papaya juice, pinch of nutmeg in curd. Soak meat pieces in curd for 3 or 4 hours. Stick all the pieces of meat on iron rod and put in medium heat of tandoor and grill in it until dry and tender. Heat little ghee in frying pan and then fry meat pieces for a few minutes, Serve at tea or at dinner.

BOTI KABABS — serves 6

1 kg lean mutton (without bones)
1 tsp red chilli powder
2 tsps ginger
4 green cardamoms
ghee for shallow frying
$1/2$ tsp orange colour
$1/2$ cup curd
salt to tast
6 garlic flakes
$1/2$ tsp cuminseeds (ground)

Cook the mutton pieces with 2 cups water on slow fire till $3/4$ tender and dry. Mix red chilli powder, ground cumin, crushed green cardamoms, salt, colour ground garlic and ginger in curd. Soak mutton species in curd for 1 hour. Pack tightly the meat pieces on metal skewers leaving the ends free for roasting on open fire or grilling till dry. Fry the roasted meat pieces in shallow ghee for a few minutes at the time of serving. Serve it hot at tea.

HUSSANI KABABS — serves 6

$1/2$ kg ribs with bones
2 tsps ginger chopped
6 tsps vinegar
2 tsps cuminseeds powder
breadcrumbs for coating
salt to taste
4 garlic flakes
1 tsp coriander
1 tsp red chilli powder
4 green cardamoms
1 egg
ghee for frying

Grind garlic, ginger and then mix red chilli powder, salt and cumin powder and rub it on the ribs and cook with 2 or 3 cups of water on slow fire till tender and dry. Cool and dip in beaten egg and coat with breadcrumbs; fry in hot ghee till golden brown. Serve hot with mint chutney at tea.

KASHMIRI KABABS — serves 6

250 gms minced meat
1 tsp cuminseeds
1 big cardamom
$1 1/2$ cups milk
2 green chillies
salt to taste
4 garlic flakes
1 tsp chopped ginger
2 cloves
1 small piece of cinnamon
2 tsps chopped coriander leaves
1 white of egg
ghee for deep frying

Cook all the above together except the white of egg and ghee till tender and dry. Cool and grind finely. Make long shaped balls and dip into white of egg and fry till golden brown. Serve at tea with mint chutney.

NARGASI KABABS *serves 6*

$1/2$ kg minced meat
2 green cardamoms
2 tsps cuminseeds
salt to taste
2 tsps chopped ginger
$1/4$ cup milk
ghee for frying

$1/2$ cup curd
$1/4$ tsp nutmeg
3 green chillies
4 garlic flakes
breadcrumbs for coating
1 egg

Cook minced meat with all the ground spices, curd, chopped garlic and ginger and one cup of water till tender and dry. Then grind it finely. Mix $1/4$ cup of milk. Dip into egg and coat with breadcrumbs and fry in hot ghee till golden brown. Serve at tea with mint chutney.

SHAMI KABABS *serves 6*

340 gms minced meat
1 small chopped onion
3 cloves
6 garlic flakes
3 green chillies
green coriander leaves
2 big cardamoms
salt to taste

127 gms chana dal
6 pieces of fresh ginger
$2^{1}/_{4}$ tsps white cumin-seeds
2 egg yolks
1 small piece of cinnamon
$1/2$ tsp red chilli powder
ghee for shallow frying

Cook minced meat and chana dal with onion, ginger, cloves, cuminseeds, green chillies, coriander leaves, cinnamon, red chilli, cardamoms, garlic and enough water till tender and water is absorbed, remove from fire, cool and grind finely. Mix salt, egg yolks and then form flat round balls and fill in each the filling.

Filling
3 onions
green coriander leaves
3 green chillies

Chop finely onions, green chillies and coriander leaves, and then fill in kababs. Fry in shallow ghee. Drain on paper. Serve hot with mint chutney.

SEEKH KABABS   serves 6

340 gms minced meat
green coriander leaves
6 ginger pieces
$1/2$ tsp red chilli
1 or 2 egg yolks
salt to taste

4 or 5 green chillies
5 garlic flakes
1 onion (medium)
1 tsp ground spices
3 tsps white cuminseeds

Grind finely green chillies, garlic flakes, ginger and onion, white cuminseeds, mix into minced meat and grind. Mix beaten eggs and ground spices salt into minced meat. Now pack tightly minced meat on iron rods or metal skewers leaving the ends and grill over a charcoal fire or in moderate tandoor or on open fire until light brown. Serve hot with mint chutney.

Mint Chutney

2 heaped tsps of tamarind (without stones and fibres)
4 green chillies

handful of fresh mint
salt to taste
coriander leaves

Soak the tamarind till soft. Pass it through a sieve. Mix it into ground fresh mint leaves and green chillies. Mix salt, serve with seekh kababs.

SHIKAM PURI KABABS   serves 6

$1/2$ kg minced lean meat
4 flakes of garlic
3 fresh green chillies
1 or 2 eggs
4 almonds
a very small piece of cinnamon
2 cardamoms
1 tsp cuminseeds
56 gms fresh coconut

1 onion
2 inch piece of ginger
4 tsps chopped green coriander leaves
1 tsp chironjee
3 cloves
1 tsp of channa flour (besan)
salt to taste
56 gms curd

mint leaves
ghee to fry
1½ cup dry breadcrumbs

Chop onion, garlic, ginger and chilli very finely and fry in ghee until light brown. Grind green coriander leaves, almonds, chironjee, cinnamon, cardamoms and cloves and mix into channa flour. Fry onion, garlic and ginger till golden in colour, mix channa flour. Then add minced meat, salt and one tbsp of coconut milk and cook until water of meat is absorbed. Turn out the contents and grind this mixture into a fine paste. Strain the curd through a coarse duster until it becomes dry. Blend together curd and ground fresh mint with a pinch of salt. Take sufficient meat paste to form a ball, the size of a billiard ball, and depress this ball gradually in the palm of your hand until you produce a shallow depression in which place a little curd mixture. Then gradually work the meat upwards until the curd is covered completely and have a round flat cutlet. Roll up cutlet into breadcrumbs. Fry golden brown in hot ghee.

(How to make coconut milk: Grind coconut finely, add 1½ tbsps of water and mix well. Strain through a muslin cloth, and then use in kababs).

POTATO KABABS STUFFED WITH MEAT

serves 6

½ kg potatoes
⅛ cup milk
salt to taste
ghee to fry

14 gms butter
½ tsp red chilli
dry breadcrumbs
1 egg

Boil and mash potatoes, add butter, milk, salt and red chilli and mix. Cook for 3 minutes. Remove from fire and cool. Take sufficient potatoes paste and from into a square shape. Fill in it cooked minced meat and shape it triangular. Beat egg with a little water, using a little flour on the kababs, dip into beaten egg and roll in dry breadcrumbs. Fry golden brown in deep in ghee. Serve hot with curd chutney.

Filling

112 gms minced meat	1 medium onion
3 slices singer	2 green chillies
2 tsps chopped coriander leaves	1 tsp flour
	$1/4$ tsp red chilli
$1/4$ tsp turmeric	1 tsp ghee
salt to taste	$1/2$ small tomato

Fry chopped onion and ginger golden brown. Add chopped tomato, green chilli, coriander leaves, turmeric and a little water and stir for 2 minutes. Add minced meat, salt, red chilli and $1/2$ cup of water; cook until tender and dry, mix one tsp of flour and cook for two minutes. Remove from fire, cool and fill in the kababs.

MUTTON KABABS *serves 8*

$1/2$ kg minced meat	1 small onion
5 garlic flakes	3 green chillies
2 bread slices (soak in water and squeeze out the water)	$1 1/2$ egg
	ghee for deep frying
	salt to taste
3 tsps breadcrumbs	1 tsp coriander leaves (chopped)
$1/4$ tsp black pepper	
breadcrumbs for coating	

Cook minced meat, chopped onion, green chilli, garlic flakes with $1 1/2$ cups of water till tender and dry. Mix soaked bread slices, coriander leaves, salt, black pepper, dry breadcrumbs (3 tsps) and $1/2$ beaten egg. Dip into beaten egg mixed with 3 tsps water. Roll in breadcrumbs. Deep fry in hot ghee till golden brown. Serve hot at tea.

PORK SEEKH KABABS *serves 6*

$1/2$ kg pork leg meat with very little fat (minced)	2 tsps ground spices
	6 garlic flakes
2 small onions	2 green chillies
$1/2$ tsp red chilli	3 tsps coarsely ground cuminseeds
2 small eggs	
4 tsps chopped coriander leaves	

Chop the onions, green chillies and coriander, Wash and dry with duster, Grind garlic finely. Mix chopped, ground garlic, spices, chillies and yolk of eggs into minced pork. Pack tightly on iron rod and then grill on the fire till dry and light brown. If the mixture is sticky, then mix roasted channa flour. Sufficient for 10 persons (22 seekh kababs). Serve at tea or dinner with mint chutney.

Mint Chutney

1 bunch of mint leaves
2 green chillies
salt to taste

$1/2$ tea cup tamarind
$1/2$ tsp ground chillies
1 tsp sugar

Soak tamarind in $3/4$ cup of water. Then pass it through sieve. Mix all the ground ingredients, salt and sugar.

LIVER KABABS *serves 6*

$1/2$ kg mutton liver
6 garlic flakes
$1/2$ tsp red chilli powder
salt to taste

1 tsp ginger
$1/2$ cup curd
1 tsp ground cuminseeds
$1/2$ cup ghee

Cut liver into small pieces, grind garlic and ginger. Mix red chilli powder, salt, ground garlic and ginger, and cumin powder into curd and add liver and soak for an hour. Pierce liver with a skewer and place on live coal till a little dry and tender or grill in oven. Smear with ghee and keep turning for 6 minutes. Serve at tea.

CHOPS AND TIKKAS

FISH CHOPS

serves 4

½ kg pomfret or sole fish
3 green chillies
salt to taste
1 egg
juice of ½ small lemon
1½ cups dry breadcrumbs
1 small onion
½ tsp black pepper
1 tsp chopped coriander leaves
ghee for shallow frying

Clean and remove the bones of fish, wash and then dry it. Mince the fish, then in it mix chopped onion, green chillies, black pepper, lemon juice and salt. Make 4 big round balls and then flatten them. Dip in beaten egg and roll in breadcrumbs. Fry in shallow ghee until golden brown. Serve hot at lunch or dinner with potato wafers. Garnish with mint leaves.

DAHI CHOPS

serves 6

450 gms mutton ribs with meat
2 tsps ginger
4 cardamoms
½ tsp red chilli powder
¼ tsp nutmeg
1 cup curd
2 tsps papaya juice
6 garlic flakes
salt to taste
ghee for frying (very shallow ghee)

Mix together ground garlic, ginger cardamoms, red chilli powder, papaya juice, and curd. Then in it soak chopped mutton ribs and keep aside for 15 minutes. Fry in very shallow ghee till golden brown and tender. Serve with mint chutney.

GOANESE MUTTON CHOPS serves 6

450 gms mutton ribs (chopped)
1 small piece of cinnamon
salt to taste
1 big cardamom
3 pieces ginger
1 sliced onion

Put all the above with water in a vessel and cook until tender and dry. Take out the spices from chops and keep aside. Now grind the following spices:

1 small piece of cinnamon
4 green cardamoms
1 small piece of mace
1 or 2 eggs
2 cloves
$1/2$ tsp red chilli powder

Sprinkle ground spices, and red chilli powder on the mutton chops. Beat egg lightly then dip the chops in it. Fry in shallow ghee until light brown on all sides. Serve hot at lunch or dinner with mint chutney.

MUTTON CHOPS serves 6

250 gms finely minced meat
12 garlic flakes
3 green chillies
$1 1/2$ tsps mustard powder
salt to taste
6 tsps dry breadcrumbs
225 gms breadcrumbs
5 mutton ribs
1 egg
1 onion
3 bread slices (soak in water, then squeeze out the liquid)
1 egg (for coating chops)
ghee to fry

Grind garlic, green chillies and onion finely. Mix the minced meat, soaked bread slices, mustard powder, salt, 6 tsps dry breadcrumbs, ground onion, green chillies, garlic and one egg. Make round balls of minced meat, in it fix mutton ribs and flatten the minced meat balls with knife. Spread the beaten eggs on both sides of chops and roll in breadcrumbs. Deep fry in ghee, first on strong fire and then slow fire. Drain on paper. Serve hot with tomato ketchup.

MUTTON CHOPS WITH GRAVY serves 6

Gravy

4 tsps flour	$2\frac{1}{2}$ cups of milk
$\frac{1}{4}$ cup of cream	1 chopped onion
3 green chillies	1 tsp chilli powder
2 tsps ghee (pure)	6 tsps tomato ketchup
a few coriander leaves	salt to taste

Heat ghee. Then fry chopped onion, green chillies and flour until light brown. Then add milk and cook a little thick. Add cream, salt, coriander leaves and stir for a few minutes.

Chops

340 gms minced meat	6 rib bones
2 green chillies	salt to taste
$\frac{1}{2}$ chopped onion	a few coriander leaves
3 bread slices (soaked)	1 egg
breadcrumbs	ghee for frying

Mix all the of chops into minced meat except ghee, breadcrumbs and egg. Shape into chops with ribs bones on breadcrumbs. Then dip into beaten eggs and roll in breadcrumbs. First fry in hot ghee and then on slow fire until brown. Drain on paper and then pour the boiling gravy on it.

MUGHLAI CHOPS serve 6

$\frac{1}{2}$ ribs with meat (chopped)	salt to taste
	2 tsps cumin powder
$\frac{1}{4}$ tsp big cardamoms	$\frac{1}{4}$ tsp nutmeg
3 green cardamoms	$\frac{1}{8}$ tsp mace
$\frac{1}{2}$ cup curd	ghee for deep frying (very shallow ghee)

Cook the meat with ribs till $\frac{3}{4}$ tender. Grind all the spices finely with a little water (6 tsps) and mix in curd. Soak the ribs with salt in curd for 25 minutes. Then fry in ghee till golden brown. Serve with chutney.

SINDHI CHOPS serve 6

6 mutton ribs (chopped)
2 tsps papaya juice
salt to taste
ghee for shallow frying
2 eggs

1 tsp amchoor
  (ground dry mango)
$1^1/_2$ tsps black pepper
$^1/_4$ tsp turmeric

Rub all the ingredients on mutton ribs. Put mutton ribs in frying pan with 3 cups of water and cover it with lid, place weight on it and cook it on very slow fire until tender and water is absorbed. Dip into beaten eggs and then fry in shallow ghee. Serve with mint chutney at lunch or dinner.

FRIED PORK CHOPS serves 4

4 pork chops
8 tsps vinegar
1 level tsp salt
3 tsps raw papaya juice
  or $^1/_2$ tsp tendering powder

2 level tsps ground spices
1 tsp pepper
ghee for shallow frying

Peel the papaya, then grind it finely and take out its juice. Make a paste of spices, papaya juice, vinegar, black pepper and salt. Beat the chops, then soak in the paste for half an hour. Heat ghee in frying pan and fry chops on slow fire until light brown and tender. Serve with grilled tomatoes.

Grill Tomatoes

340 gms tomatoes
salt to taste
1 or $1^1/_2$ tsps ghee

1 tsp ground spices
2 tsps vinegar

Cut the thin slices from the both ends of tomatoes. Heat ghee and fry it with vinegar, salt and spices until half cooked. Serve with fried pork chops.

MULTANI CHOPS serves 6

8 pork chops
4 garlic flakes or $^1/_2$ level
  tsp garlic powder
1 tsp ground cuminseeds
3 tsps papaya juice or
  $^1/_2$ tsp tendering powder

$^3/_4$ cup curd
$^1/_2$ tsp red chilli powder
2 tsps fresh ginger
salt to taste
1 kitchen tsp ghee

Beat the chops with knife and wash them. Make paste or curd, papaya juice, ground garlic, ginger, red chilli powder, cumin powder and salt and rub cover the chops. Keep aside for 15 minutes and then fry in ghee till golden brown. Serve with tomato slices and lemon at lunch or dinner.

CHOPS IN TOMATO   serve 8

10 pork chops
2 green chillies or
   $1/2$ tsp white pepper
1 cup tomato pulp or puree
6 tsps chopped onion
4 tsps ghee
salt to taste
4 tsps tomato ketchup

Beat out the chops with rolling pin, then wash them. Heat ghee, fry chops and onion till golden brown, add green chilli, salt and one cup of water, cook till tender and dry. Add tomato ketchup and tomato pulp and cook till a little dry. Serve at lunch or dinner.

CHICKEN TIKKA   serves 6

See the recipe for Tandoori Chicken. Same ingredients. Cut chicken into small pieces and then marinate in curd mixture for two hours. Pack it tightly on iron skewer, 10 inch long, leaving the ends free. Roast in tandoor or wire rack in moderate oven until dry and tender. Baste them frequently with ghee. Serve hot with lemon slices at dinner.

FISH TIKKA   serves 6

454 gms fish or mackerel
3 small pieces of fresh ginger
6 green cardamoms
3 or 4 tsps curd
salt to taste
15 garlic flakes
$1 1/2$ tsp red chilli powder
$1/4$ tsp cinnamon powder
1 small piece of mace
$1/2$ tsp orange colour

Wash the fish without bones, then dry with cloth. Cut into medium pieces, grind garlic and ginger finely. Grind all the spices. Mix all the ground ingredients, colour salt the red chilli powder into curd. Rub on the fish pieces and keep for one hour. Stick on iron rod, then put on medium fire of charcoal, or on grill, turn them frequently or grill until nicely browned. Serve with mint chutney at tea.

MUTTON TIKKA   serves 6

$1/2$ kg mutton without   20 garlic flakes
   bones (from leg portion) $1/4$ tsp orange colour
   or two undercuts   3 tsps raw papaya juice
2 tsps curd $1 1/2$ tsps red chilli powder
2 tsps cuminseeds   1 tsp ground ginger
salt to taste

Grind garlic and ginger and cuminseeds finely. Then in it mix salt, papaya juice, colour, curd, red chilli powder and rub on the meat pieces and keep for 35 minutes. Grill them on the fire till dry. They fry in shallow ghee. Serve with lemon slices and mint chutney. (Boil mutton pieces in two cups of water till $3/4$ tender and dry. Cool. Rub all the above ingredients.)

PORK TIKKA   serves 6

$1/2$ kg lean pork or 3 undercuts

See the recipe for Mutton Tikka.
Same ingredients and methods as for Mutton Tikka.

PAKORAS

CHICKEN PAKORA
serves 6

1 small chicken
$1/2$ tsp thymol seeds
$1/2$ tsp red chilli powder
$1/2$ tsp ground cumin
1 tsp salt
3 tsps amchoor (dry mango powder)

Boil chicken in two cups of water till tender and dry. Remove bones. Rub cumin, thymol seeds, salt and red chilli powder on chicken pieces and keep aside till batter is prepared.

Pakora Batter
2 cups gram flour
$1/4$ tsp ground red chilli
ghee for deep frying
$1/2$ tsp baking powder
salt to taste
water of batter

Beat gram flour with a little water till it floats on the surface of water when tested in 1 cup water. Make thick batter. Mix salt, red chilli, and baking powder. Dip chicken pieces and fry them golden brown and crisp. Sprinkle special masala on pakoras or serve with mint chutney.

Special Masala
3 tsps ground cuminseeds
2 tsps salt
4 tsps amchoor (dry mango powder)
1 tsp red chilli powder
1 tsp black pepper

Mix all the ground spices together. Keep in a glass jar. Sprinkle on pakoras at the time of serving.

Mint Chutney
For ingredients and method see earlier recipe for Pork Seekh Kabab.

EGG PAKORA
serves 8

6 full boiled eggs   6 tsps special masala

Cut eggs into 4 pieces lengthwise. Rub special masala over them. Dip in gram flour, batter and fry till golden brown and crisp. Serve with mint chutney at tea.
(Pakora batter in this case has to be prepared as given in the recipe for Chicken Pakora).

BRAIN PAKORA
serves 6

3 brains   1 cup of besan
3 tsps vinegar   salt to taste
ghee for frying $1/2$ level tsp baking powder

Wash the brains 3 or 4 times. Boil 3 cups of water with 1 tsp salt and vinegar and in it cook the brains for a few minutes (till firm). Put it on the strainer so that the water may trickle down. Beat the besan with hand till it floats on the surface of the water. Mix a little water to make a thick dropping consistency. Mix salt and baking powder and $1/4$ tsp red chilli powder. Dip the medium pieces of brain in the batter and fry in hot ghee on medium fire till golden brown. Then sprinkle special masala at the time of serving.

FISH PAKORA
serves 8

250 gms fish (without $1/2$ tsp thymol seeds
  bones and skin) $1/4$ cup vinegar
6 garlic flakes $1/2$ tsp red chilli powder
$1/2$ tsp chopped ginger   1 tsp salt

Wash the small pieces of fish without bones, dry with duster. Make a paste of vinegar, ground garlic and ginger, red chilli powder, salt and thymol seeds. Rub it over the fish pieces and keep aside for 15 minutes till batter is ready.
(For pakora batter same recipe as given earlier for Chicken Pakoras.)
Beat gram flour with a little water till it floats on the surface of water when tested in one cup of water.

SNACKS

MUTTON SAMOSAS   serves 12

Filling
225 gms minced meat
1 tsp ground spices
$1/2$ or $1/4$ tsp ground red chilli
salt to taste
2 tsps flour
2 tsps chopped onion

2 green chillies
1 tsp ground cumin seeds
1 tsp chopped ginger
few coriander leaves
113 gms peas (boiled)
1 tsp ghee

Cook the minced meat with one cup of water, onions, ginger, ground red chilli and salt till it becomes dry. Heat two tsps ghee in it, fry flour till it is very slightly golden brown. Mix minced meat, coriander leaves and all the leftover spices. Fill it in the samosas.

Dough
170 gms flour
9 or 10 tsps water
ghee for frying

9 tsps melted ghee
$3/4$ tsp salt

Knead the flour, melted ghee, water and salt till it is smooth. Then cover it with a wet cloth for at least 35 minutes (in summer for 15 mts). Then make round balls. Roll out very thin into rounds and then cut each into half. Wet it on the outside at the bottom with water. Turn it from one side, then the other and make a shape of a cone or samosa. Fill the filling and close it. Fry in hot ghee on medium heat till golden brown. Put it on the strainer so that ghee may trickle down. Serve at tea.

MEAT PIE   serves 6

340 gms minced meat
$1/2$ tsp black pepper

1 tsp ground spices
85 gms butter

1/4 cup cream
3 eggs
small onion
grated cheese
salt to taste

28 gms flour
1 tsp chopped coriander leaves
2 fresh green chillies

Fry onion in 1 oz butter until light brown, add minced meat, 1 cup water, black pepper, ground spices, chopped coriander leaves and green chillies and cook until dry. Remove from fire and keep aside. Cream the butter and add yolks, cream and $1/2$ oz flour and beat. Beat egg whites until stiff, then fold in the remaining flour and 1 oz grated cheese and yolk mixture lightly. Pour half of the egg mixture into greased pie dish and then spread cooked minced meat. Spread the remaining half of the egg mixture on top. Bake it (in 350° F) until set and light brown on the top. Serve hot at lunch or dinner with tomato ketchup.

FISH ROLLS   serves 6

8 thin pieces of fish
1 level tsp black pepper
1 onion
1 or 2 eggs
1 hard boiled egg
1/4 tsp cinnamon powder
1 tsp ground spices
1 cup dry breadcrumbs

juice of $1/2$ lemon
$1/2$ cup water
2 small pieces of fresh ginger
3 small tomatoes
2 green chillies
ghee for frying
salt to taste

Beat 12 oz fish without bones with flat knife until it becomes thin. Then rub salt, lemon juice and $1/2$ tsp pepper on it and keep it aside. Boil 4 oz fish with 1 tsp salt, $1/2$ tsp and $1/2$ cup water in a vessel until tender, and the water is evaporated. Cool, then chop it finely or mash it. Chop onion, boiled egg, green chilli, ginger and tomatoes without pulp. Mix ground spices, salt, $1/2$ tsp pepper and chopped ingredients into the chopped fish. Spread this mixture on each of the 6 fish pieces and roll up carefully and fasten with toothpicks. Beat eggs with a little salt and one tbsp water. Dip the fish rolls into the beaten eggs and then roll in breadcrumbs. Heat ghee in frying pan on medium fire and drop the fish rolls carefully. Fry until brown. Drain on paper. Remove the toothpicks and serve hot with tomato ketchup.

GOANESE FISH IN TOMATO SAUCE serves 6

454 gms fish
1 tsp four
$1/2$ tsp white pepper

140 gms butter
salt to taste

Tomato Sauce

340 gms tomatoes
2 cloves
$1/2$ tsp red chilli powder
2 garlic cloves
$1/2$ inch piece of cinnamon
salt to taste

2 tsps chopped coriander leaves
2 capsicum (green sweet chillies)
1 spring onion
2 small pieces of ginger

Remove bones and skin of the fish, wash and then dry it. Rub salt and pepper and then dust with flour. Melt butter and fry fish lightly. Keep aside. Put chopped tomatoes, spring onion, garlic, ginger, coriander leaves, red chilli powder and whole spices in a vessel and cook until thick and tomatoes are tender. Pass through a sieve. Mix big slices of capsicum into sauce and boil. In it mix fish lightly. Serve hot at lunch or dinner.

FRIED FISH (Punjabi Style) serves 6

680 gms fish (Singhara)
3 or 4 tsps red chilli powder
$1/4$ tsp orange colour
1 onion
20 garlic flakes for flavouring the oil

salt to taste
3 or 4 tsps ground dry mango
besan for coating
$1/2$ tsp orange colour
mustard oil for deep frying

Wash the fish and then dry it. Rub all the ingredients and colour except besan. Coat with besan. Keep for two hours. Heat oil and then fry garlic flakes and onion until brown, remove from the oil and throw them away. Fry fish until light brown. Take it out from oil and keep it for a few minutes and then again fry it until nicely browned. Serve hot at lunch, tea or dinner.

FRIED FISH WITH SPICES   serves 6

454 gms fish (singhara)
2 tsps white cuminseeds
$1/2$ tsp red chilli powder
salt to taste
ghee for deep frying
$1 1/2$ cups dry breadcrumbs
2 cloves
1 inch piece of cinnamon
$1/2$ tsp black pepper
$1/2$ lemon juice
1 or 2 eggs

Wash the fish well and then dry it with cloth. Rub salt, lemon juice, ground spices, red chilli powder and black pepper and keep aside for 35 minutes. Dip into beaten egg and roll in breadcrumbs. Deep fry in ghee until brown. Serve hot at dinner with potato wafers. (Fried fish with spices can be served at tea without wafers).

STUFFED POMFRET   serves 4

1 pomfret
$1/2$ tsp turmeric
2 tsps vinegar
$3/4$ tsp salt
1 tsp chilli powder

Stuffing
$1/4$ fresh coconut
  (without brown portion)
1 onion
1 tomato
1 tsp ground spices
2 green chillies
2 inch pieces of fresh ginger
2 tsps ground cuminseeds
ghee for shallow frying
salt to taste

Clean the pomfret and slit near the head on the stomach side and remove the entrails. Keep the fish whole. Mix salt, turmeric, vinegar and chilli powder and rub on the fish inside and outside with the paste. Grind all the ingredients except tomato of stuffing to a thick paste, then fry in a little ghee for 5 minutes with chopped tomato and stuff the fish well with this. Tie the pomfrets round and round with a thread to secure the stuffing. Heat a little ghee in a heavy frying pan until smoky. Place the fish in it, then cover with lid and put on low heat until golden brown. Then turn it again, cover with lid until tender and golden brown. Serve hot at lunch or dinner.

STUFFED TOMATO WITH FISH serves 6

6 medium sized tomatoes
½ small onion
1 chopped tomato
salt to taste
1 tsp chopped ginger

340 gms fish
1 tsp ground spices
2 green chillies
2 tsps tomato ketchup
¼ tsp black pepper
1 tsps ghee

Wash and dry the tomatoes and then scoop out the pulp and keep it aside. Boil the fish in salted water until tender. Cool and then mash coarsely. Fry chopped onion, green chillies and ginger until light brown, add chopped tomato, mashed fish, ground spices, salt, black pepper, ketchup, tomato pulp and stir it for a few minutes until dry. Fill in tomatoes and bake in slow over until skin is tender, or fry it in shallow ghee lightly. Garnish with mint leaves. Serve at lunch or dinner.

TANDOORI FISH serves 8

1 hilsa fish (907 gms)
14 gms ginger
½ tsp orange colour
3 ground cloves
3 tsps curd
3 or 4 tsps chilli powder

20 garlic flakes
¼ level tsp ground cinnamon
1 small piece of mace
2 tsps ground dry mango
salt to taste

Clean and remove the entrails of fish and then wash the fish. Keep the fish whole. Dry with clean cloth. Grind garlic and ginger finely and then in it mix ground cinnamon, cloves, mace, dry mango, colour, salt, chilli powder and curd. Rub it on the fish and keep it aside for 15 minutes. Stick the whole fish on iron skewer, 2 feet long and put in tandoor until dry and tender. Now baste it frequently with ghee until light brown. Squeeze juice of one lemon to taste over the fish before serving. Serve hot at dinner. (Hilsa fish without skewer can be grilled in oven on wire rack; baste it frequently until dry and tender. Glaze with ghee and keep it in oven for a few minutes.)

TOMATO FISH
serves 8

340 gms fish
ghee to fry
$3/4$ tsp white pepper
112 gms tomatoes
3 tsps sugar
6 tsps tomato ketchup
1 big onion
3 tsps lemon juice
$1 1/2$ tsps salt
flour to coat the fish
1 tbsp ghee

Wash the fish and dry it with duster, cut into big pieces, sprinkle lemon juice and $3/4$ tsp salt and keep aside for 5 minutes. Now coat the fish with flour and fry in shallow ghee until light brown. Remove from ghee. Now fry chopped onion in one tbsp ghee until golden brown, add chopped tomatoes, salt, sugar, white pepper and tomato ketchup and cook for a few minutes. Add fried fish and cook for five minutes. Serve hot at lunch or dinner. (Before chopping the tomatoes, put in boiling water for 5 minutes and then peel it.)

HAM AND POTATO BALLS
serves 8

$1/2$ kg potatoes
14 gms flour
salt and pepper to taste
ghee to fry
170 gms cooked ham
1 or 2 eggs
Dry breadcrumbs for coating

Boil the potatoes, mash and combine with cooked ham finely minced. Add salt, black pepper and yolk of an egg and mix it. Form into cutlet shape, use a little flour, dip them into beaten egg and roll in breadcrumbs. Fry golden brown Decorate with green coriander leaves. Serve hot.

FRIED SAUSAGES
serves 6

$1/2$ kg small sized sausages
5 tsps butter
$1/4$ tsp white pepper
3 cloves
1 bay leaf
salt to taste for tomatoes
ghee to fry
$1/2$ kg peas
salt to taste for peas
2 tsps chopped coriander leaves
2 tsps sugar
$1/4$ tsp red chilli powder

Boil peas in 1 tsp soda bicarbonate for 4 minutes. Remove the vessel from the fire and keep peas in covered vessel till soft. Fry in butter and add salt and pepper.

Prick sausages with a needle and place in frying pan. Cover with water and cook until all the water has evaporated. Brown them in their own fat. Drain on paper and then cook in tomato sauce for 5 minutes. Place fried peas on bottom of oval shaped dish and place sausages with sauce over them. Serve for lunch or dinner.

For tomato sauce, chop tomatoes, coriander leaves, onion and cook with red chilli powder, bay leaves, cloves, salt and sugar until tender and a little thick. Strain and serve.

STUFFED POTATO SAUSAGES

340 gms potatoes
2 tsps white jeera
a few coriander leaves
salt to taste
ghee for frying

16 sausages
2 green chillies
1 beaten egg
breadcrumbs for coating

Boil the potatoes in salted water till tender. Cool and grate. Mix green chillies, coriander leaves, salt and white jeera with the potatoes.

Prick the sausages and then cook in 1 cup of water till dry and then fry them in their fat. Fill in the grated potatoes and dip into beaten egg and coat with breadcrumbs. Decorate with lettuce leaves, beetroot and raddish. Serve at lunch or dinner.

CHICKEN PICKLE   serves 8

1 kg chicken pieces
3 tsps ground ginger
250 gms lemon
4 ground cloves
4 tsps ground coriander
   seeds
2 cups mustard oil

20 garlic flakes
1 cup vinegar
2 tsps red chilli powder
1 tsp ground cinnamon
3 tsps aniseeds
$1/_2$ tsp ground nutmeg
8 tsps ground cuminseeds

Boil the chicken pieces till tender, put on a strainer so that water may trickle down. Heat oil till smoky, then fry chicken pieces till light brown. Remove the chicken pieces from the oil and fry ground garlic and ginger till light brown. Add vinegar, red chilli powder, coriander, aniseed, cumin, salt, lemon juice, vinegar nutmeg and chicken pieces and cook for 10 minutes. Remove from the fire, cool then put them in a jar. (Chicken pickle can be kept for one month).

MEAT PICKLE   serves 8

$1^1/_2$ kg pork
$1^1/_2$ onion
$1^1/_2$ cup mustard oil
4 lemons
salt to taste
$1/_2$ tsp ground cardamoms
1 tsp ground cinnamon
3 tsps ground dry coriander

70 gms garlic
70 gms ginger
2 cups vinegar
4 tsps red chillies
4 tsps ground white cuminseeds
$3/_4$ tsp ground cloves

Boil meat in salted water until tender and then strain it. Heat oil, fry meat until light brown and take it out from the oil. Fry ground onion, garlic and ginger until light brown. Add vinegar, lemon juice, red chilli powder, ground spices, salt and meat and stir for a few minutes. Cool and then put in jar and keep for one day and then serve at lunch or dinner. (Pickle can be kept for a month.)

CHEESE TOAST   serves 6

$1/_2$ cup flour
4 eggs
4 butter
$1/_2$ tsp salt
$1/_2$ tsp red chilli powder
6 or 8 slices bread

$1/_2$ cup cheese
$1/_4$ cup water
$1/_2$ tsp baking powder
$1/_2$ tsp white pepper
$1/_4$ tsp mustard powder

Boil water with butter, add the flour and stir on fire until it leaves the sides of pan. Cool the mixture, beat eggs one by one. Now add salt, white pepper, red chilli powder, mustard powder, grated cheese and baking powder and mix it nicely. Spread it on one side of the bread slices and then deep fry in ghee on medium fire until light brown. Remove from ghee and cut into rectangular shape and then again fry until nicely browned. Drain on paper and serve hot at tea with tomato ketchup.

EGG IN TOMATO ON TOAST *serves 6*

6 medium sized tomatoes
1/2 cup melted butter
salted butter
6 tsps grated cheese
6 very small eggs
salt and white pepper to taste
6 bread slices

Scoop out the pulp from tomatoes. Pour 1 tsp melted butter in each tomato, in it break one egg, pour butter, sprinkle salt and pepper, cover the tomato hole with grated cheese and bake till cheese is golden brown and tomato is a little tender, put on buttered toast. Serve at breakfast.

SCRAMBLED EGGS ON TOAST *serves 2*

4 tsp butter
1/4 cup cream
2 green chillies
4 bread slices
2 eggs
3 tsps chopped onion
salt to taste
salted butter for toast

Chop green chillies and onion. Beat eggs, and salt. Mix onion and green chillies and butter into eggs, stir on slow fire in heavy pan till thick. Put it on buttered toast and serve at breakfast.

CHEESE OMELETTE SOUFFLE *serves 2*

2 eggs
2 tsps craft cheese
1 tsp chopped parsley leaves or fresh coriander leaves
3 tsps ghee
salt to taste
1 green chilli
1/4 tsp white pepper

Separate the yolks from whites of two eggs and put yolks in small bowl, add white pepper, salt, chopped green chilli and coriander. Beat with a wooden spoon until creamy and mix one tbsp grated cheese. Whip the whites to a stiff froth and fold them lightly into the yolks. Melt ghee in frying pan, pour the mixture and stir on the surface until it beings to set. Sprinkle one tbsp grated cheese on the omelette. Leave until nicely browned underneath, then slip a knife under it and fold first from one side and then from the other, towards the centre. Turn on to a dish and serve immediately at breakfast.

EGG OPEN SANDWICHES
(Russian Style)   serves 6

6 bread slices $1/_4$ cup butter
6 eggs   5 tsps mayonnaise sauce
a few parsley leaves $1/_4$ tsp salt

Make a smooth paste of butter and salt. Cut the slices into round shape with water glass. Poach the egg till hard. Spread butter paste on slices and on them put poached eggs and spread mayonnaise sauce and sprinkle parsley leaves.

RUSSIAN SANDWICHES   serves 10

$1/_2$ cup butter $1/_2$ or $3/_4$ cup cream
1 kg bread   cheese
$1/_4$ tsp chilli powder $1/_4$ tsp salt
1 tsp mustard powder   3 boiled eggs

Mix together butter, cream cheese, salt, chilli powder and mustard powder to a soft paste. Mash boiled eggs. Cut bread lengthwise in slices and $1/_4$ inch thick. Spread soft paste with flat knife and then mashed eggs. Wrap each roll in butter paper. Fasten with toothpicks and chill. When ready to serve slice about $1/_4$ inch thick. Serve at tea.

INDIAN PUDDINGS

BREAD PUDDING serves 8

10 bread slices
2 eggs
1 tsp kewara flavour
1/2 cup butter
2 cups milk
1/2 cup of sugar
jam or jelly

Spread butter on slices and put two slices together by spreading a little jam, arrange them in greased pudding dish. Beat egg, milk, sugar and kewara flavour together Pour over the slices and keep it till milk is absorbed. Bake (temp. 350°) till golden brown. Serve hot.

EGG HALWA serves 6

8 egg yolks
4 crushed green cardamoms
1/4 cup pistachio
3/4 cup ghee
4 egg whites
1/2 cup sugar
1/4 cup peeled almond
silver leaves for decoration

Beat yolks, sugar and egg whites lightly. Heat ghee, add beaten eggs and stir on slow fire until it leaves the sides of pan. Remove from fire. Decorate with silver leaves, chopped pistachio and almonds, serve hot at lunch or dinner.

JALEBI PUDDING serves 6

2 cups (heaped) jalebis
1 cup milk
2 silver leaves
2 eggs
1/2 tsp kewara flavour
1 tsp chopped peeled almond

Grease pudding dish with butter. Arrange jalebis in it. Beat eggs, milk and kewara flavour and pour it over the jalebis. Bake (350° F) till set and golden brown from top. Remove from oven, spread silver leaves over it and sprinkle with chopped almonds.

INDIAN ROYAL PUDDING　　　　　　serves 6

3/4 cup khoya　　　　　　2 eggs
3/4 cup sugar　　　　　　1/3 cup ghee
1/2 cup flour　　　　　　1/2 tsp baking powder
1 tsp kewara flavour　　2 tsps almonds
1 tsp pistachio　　　　　2 tsps raisins

Cream the chilled ghee and sugar until fluffy, add yolks of eggs and beat it. Mix mashed khoya, sifted flour and baking powder. Beat egg whites until stiff. Mix peeled and chopped almonds, raisins, pistachio and kewara flavour into egg mixture and then fold whites of eggs lightly. Grease the loaf tin and dust with flour, then pour in mixture and do not fill more than two-thirds full. Bake in moderate oven (350°F) for about 45 minutes until light brown. Insert a wooden pick; if it comes out smoothly cool the mixture and put in a dish. Pour the hot cornflour custard on baked pudding and cover it.

Cornflour Custard

2 cups milk　　　　　　　1/2 cup sugar
1/4 tsp salt　　　　　　　a few drops of yellow
2 tsps cornflour　　　　　　colour
2 egg yolks　　　　　　　pistachio for decoration
1/2 tsp kewara flavour　　3/4 cup cream

Make a paste of sugar, salt, cornflour and eggs. Boil milk, put on slow fire. Add the paste of cornflour into the milk and stir until thick. Remove from fire. Mix half the cream and kewara flavour. Pour it hot on the pudding and cool it. Now whip the rest of the cream with yellow colour and decorate custard with it and then sprinkle chopped pistachio on it.

RICE PUDDING　　　　　　　　　　serves 6

1/2 cup rice　　　　　　　2 eggs
1 cup milk　　　　　　　　1/2 cup sugar
1 tsp kewara flavour　　　2 tsps raisins

1 tsp pistachio   1 tsp almond
2 bread slices (for crumbs)

Boil rice till tender, strain it. Beat eggs, milk, sugar and kewara flavour. In egg mixture mix boiled rice, raisins, almond, pistachio. Put it in a pudding dish. Sprinkle fresh breadcrumbs over it and bake (350°F) till set and golden brown. Serve it at lunch or dinner.

SHAHI TUKRI WITH EGG   serves 8

6 bread slices
2 cups milk
$1/2$ cup khoya
1 tsp chopped peeled almond
4 green cardamoms

1 egg
$1/2$ cup sugar
1 tsp chopped pistachio
silver leaves for decoration
ghee for frying

Remove hard crust, cut into rectangular pieces. Fry in ghee till golden brown. Beat egg in milk. Mix khoya, sugar and green cardamoms in milk. Boil the milk and in it put fried bread slices, and cook till thick. Remove from fire. Arrange in a dish, decorate with silver leaves and dry nuts. Serve cold.

SOUPS

ALMOND SOUP WITH CLEAR STOCK   serves 8

Stock

250 gms mutton ribs
1 bay leaf
1 small piece of onion
12 cups of water
1 small piece of ginger
10 peppercorns
10 crushed almonds

Cook together mutton ribs with all the ingredients till quite tender and reduced to 8 cups. Now put it on the strainer. Heat the stock with crushed almonds.

Soup

12 level tsps flour
$1/3$ cup cream
white pepper to taste
3 tsps butter
1 or 2 tsp cornflour
salt to taste

Fry the flour in butter till golden brown on very slow fire. Then add stock with almonds and stir till it becomes thick but not very thick. If it is thin then mix cornflour in $1/4$ cup of water and mix it in the soup and cook till thick. Mix salt and pepper, put it in cups and mix cream (1 tsp) in each cup. Serve hot.

CLEAR SOUP   serves 8

Stock

$1/2$ kg bones of lamb or chicken
1 onion
1 potato (medium size)
3 bay leaves
15 cups (5 pints) water
2 big slices of fresh ginger

Cook all the ingredients on slow fire till quite tender. Mash and strain.

Soup

250 gms mutton
2 onions
1 big piece fresh ginger
1 tomato
$1/4$ tsp caramel syrup

8 cups stock
2 bay leaves
3 whites of eggs
5 tsps vinegar

Put whole onion on fire until dark brown. Put all the ingredients with stock and brown onions in pan and cook on strong fire until it boils. Then cook on slow fire for one hour. Do not stir the soup. Strain it. Sprinkle salt and white pepper and serve hot at lunch or dinner.

CHICKEN CREAM SOUP serves 10

Stock

250 gms chicken bones and 4 haunches of lamb
1 big onion
2 chicken breasts

3 bay leaves
1 big slice of ginger
14 cups of water
1 medium potato

Put all the ingredients in the pan and cook until the chicken breast is tender. Take out chicken breast from the stock and again cook on slow fire till the bones are quite tender. Then mash the meat and strain it.

Soup

2 pint stock (6 cups)
3 tsps butter
$1/4$ cup cream

8 level tsps flour
$1 1/2$ tsps milk
salt and pepper to taste

Melt butter in pan and fry flour for 2 minutes without browning. Add stock and cook till a little thick. Mix small pieces of boiled chicken breast, milk, salt and pepper. Put it in soup dish and mix lightly one tsp cream in each soup dish.

FRENCH ONION SOUP serves 2

$1 1/2$ medium sized onion slices (thin)
1 toast

$1/2$ level tsp white pepper
3 cups of stock
1 or 2 tsps caramel syrup

salt to taste   1 egg
3 tsps grated cheese

Fry the onion slices till golden brown. Then drain them on the paper. Take out the grease with the paper as much as you can. Now put the stock, fried onion slices, grated cheese, salt, white pepper, unbeaten egg (without shells), a full toast, caramel syrup in an earthen vessel with lid and keep it tight with kneaded flour. Bake it in the oven for 15 or 20 minutes or steam for 25 minutes. Then remove the dough and put a white napkin all around.

Stock

2 haunches   1 small potato (cut into
12 cups of water   half with peels)
1 small piece of ginger 5 peppercorns

Cook all the ingredients together, first on strong fire for about 35 minutes. Then on slow fire till it is reduced to 3 or 4 cups. Then put it on the strainer. Use it for soup.

TOMATO SOUP WITH CREAM   serves 8

Stock

250 gms mutton ribs 12 cups of water
 or haunches   1 bay leaf

Cook all the till quite tender. Strain it. Use it for soup.

Soup

$1/2$ kg tomatoes   One clove
6 cups of stock   2 tsps cornflour
salt and white pepper 3 tsps sugar
 to taste

Cook chopped tomato and clove in stock till tender and pass through a sieve and in it mix sugar, salt and white pepper. Mix cornflour in $1/2$ cup of water and stir in soup till a little thick on the fire. Remove it from the fire, mix 2 tsps cream in each cup. Serve hot with crutons (fried bread cubes).

TOMATO SOUP (Ukrainian Style)   serves 8

- 3 hunches of lamb
- 1 spring onion (chopped)
- 2 tsps sugar
- 5 tsps flour
- ½ kg tomato
- 2 tsps parsley leaves or coriander leaves
- salt to taste
- 1 carrot (chopped)
- 1 cup cabbage (chopped)
- ½ tsp white pepper
- 1 cup cooked and drained rice
- ¼ cup butter
- 10 cups of water

Cook all the vegetables and 4 haunches in water till vegetables are quite tender. Add salt, pepper, sugar and whole tomatoes and cook on low heat till tender. Pass it through a sieve. Fry flour in butter on slow fire till very light golden in colour. Mix strained soup and cook till it boils.

Put some rice in each dish, pour the hot soup over it and sprinkle coriander leaves. Serve hot.

CHICKEN, FISH, MUTTON, PORK PREPARATIONS

CHICKEN

GRILL CHICKEN
serves 4

1 chicken with skin
4 tsps salad oil
$1/2$ tsp ajino-moto
1 tsp red chilli powder

6 tsps worcestershire sauce
2 tsps salt
$1/4$ tsp mustard powder
ghee for shallow frying

Cut the chicken into half. Make a paste of worcestershire sauce, ajini-moto, chilli powder, mustard powder, salad oil and salt. Rub this on the chicken and keep it for one hour, fry $1/2$ the chicken in 3 tsps ghee until brown, and then fry the other half of the chicken in the same way. Add $1/2$ cup of water and cook for a few minutes. Take out the chicken from the gravy and put it on a wire rack. Put the round flat pie dish under the wire rack for dripping and grill in the oven (315°F) and turn it frequently until tender. Take out the chicken from the oven. Add the gravy into the dripping and mix well; if thick add a little warm water and mix well. Pour on the chicken and sever hot at lunch or dinner.

    (Chicken can be grilled in pressure cooker. Put chicken in any mould and cover with lid, cook in pressure cooker until tender. Serve hot at lunch or dinner.)

CHICKEN CHOPS
serves 2

Breast of one chicken with a little bone
$1/2$ tsp chopped onion
$1/2$ tsp black pepper

3 tsps worcestershire sauce
2 tsps salad oil
$1/2$ tsp chopped green chilli
$1/2$ cup minced chicken meat

1 beaten egg
salt to taste
ghee for shallow frying
$1/4$ tsp mustard powder
$3/4$ cup breadcrumbs

Make a paste of all the ingredients except minced chicken meat. Beat chicken breast until flat, then rub the above paste and keep it for 15 minutes. Mix salt and pepper and one tsp worcestershire sauce into minced chicken and then spread on one side of chicken chop. Spread beaten egg on it and then roll in breadcrumbs. Fry in shallow ghee until nicely browned. Serve hot with cooked spinach, peas, beans and potato strips.

Fried Spinach

$1/2$ kg spinach
1 small onion
$1/2$ tsp salt
$1/2$ tsp ajino-moto
3 tsps butter
2 garlic flakes
$1/2$ tsp soda bicarbonate
water for boiling spinach

Boil water, add $1/2$ tsp salt and soda and boil for a few minutes. Add spinach without stems and cook until tender. Remove from fire and drain. Fry chopped garlic and onion in butter. Add chopped spinach, salt and ajino-moto and fry for a few minutes.

Fried Beans

250 gms beans
$3/4$ tsp salt
water to boil the vegetables
3 tsps butter
$1/4$ tsp soda

Boil water, add salt and soda. Then add chopped beans (cut the beans in slanting direction), cover the vessel and cook until tender. Wash beans in cold water and fry in butter.

Fried Peas

Same recipe as for Beans.
Soda bicarbonate is used only to retain its green colour.

CHICKEN A-LA-KING   serves 8

4 big pieces of dry white mushrooms
$1/2$ carrot
1 bay leaf
1 tsp white pepper
2 tsp flour
6 tsps cream
6 tsps butter

$1/2$ chicken
$1 1/2$ cups milk
$1/2$ onion slices
2 small fresh ginger slices
2 tsps lemon juice
1 onion
salt to taste
2 tomatoes

Sock white mushrooms overnight and boil until tender. Cut into small pieces. Boil chicken with carrot, onion, ginger, slices, bay leaf and a little salt until tender. Remove the bones and then cut into small pieces. Take out the pulp from one tomato and cut into small pieces. Melt butter, fry very finely chopped onion until light brown, then add chicken, white mushrooms, tomato pieces, salt, pepper and flour and stir for a few minutes. Add milk and cream and cook for one minute. Remove from fire and mix lemon juice. Put in pie dish, then decorate with tomato flowers. Serve cooked beans, peas, and spinach separately.

CHICKEN A-LA-KIEV   serves 2

2 chicken breasts
1 grated bread slice
$1/2$ tsp mustard powder
ghee to fry
2 eggs
4 tsps whipped cream
$1/2$ tsp ajino-moto

1 onion
salt to taste
$1/2$ beaten egg
breadcrumbs for coating
2 green chillies
2 boiled eggs
2 tsps butter

Grind onion and green chillies finely. Mince boiled eggs. Mix whipped cream, chopped onion, green chillies, minced boiled eggs, grated bread slice, salt, $1/4$ tsp ajini-moto and butter and chill. Beat chicken breast flat and then sprinkle $1/4$ tsp ajini-moto, mustard powder, salt and beaten egg. Make a pear shape of chilled mixture and fill in the chicken breast. Dip in beaten egg and roll in breadcrumbs. Deep fry in ghee. Serve hot with fried vegetables (peas, beans, spinach). Serve hot at dinner.

CHICKEN A-LA-MEXICANO *serves 2*

Filling
3 pieces of liver
½ small onion
   (chopped finely)
6 tsps butter

2 tsps cream (whipped)
½ tsp ajino-moto
½ green chilli
¼ tsp salt

Chicken Mexicano
1 egg
⅛ tsp salt
3 tsps beaten eggs
¼ tsp mustard
½ tsp salt
ghee for deep frying
   the breadcrumbs

1 tsp ghee
2 whole pieces of one
   chicken breast
1 level tsp ajino-moto
1 or 2 eggs (for bread-
   crumbs)

Heat one tsp ghee in frying pan and make two thin omelettes. Fry liver, chopped onion and green chilli in ghee and then chop liver finely. Add whipped cream, salt and ajino-moto into chopped liver, mix it and chill. Fill the liver into chilled butter. Now beat the breast meat with sharp knife until it becomes thin and flat, and on it sprinkle mustard powder, ajino-moto and 3 tsps beaten egg. Fill the chilled butter in the omelette and then put omelette in the breast meat and make a round ball, dust with a little flour, dip in the egg and roll in breadcrumbs twice or thrice. Deep fry in ghee on strong fire until golden brown, then on slow fire. Drain on paper. (Put chicken mexicano on mashed potato and serve at dinner with cooked beans, spinach and peas.)

AMERICAN CHICKEN *serves 4*

For Frying Chicken
2 back legs of
   2 spring chicken
½ small onion
¼ tsp mustard powder
¼ tsp white pepper
2 tsps raw papaya juice
2 tsps worcestershire sauce

2 chillies
2 tsps flour
1 egg
salt to taste
ghee for frying
1 tsp water
1 cup breadcrumbs
   for coating

Chop onion and green chillies finely. Boil egg and in it mix flour, mustard powder, salt, white pepper, water, papaya juice, worcestershire sauce, chopped onion and green chillies. Put chicken in this mixture for 10 minutes. Coat with breadcrumbs and fry in pan on medium fire until golden brown and drain on paper.

For Decoration

1 onion
1 cup boiled rice
250 gms spinach
3 thin slices of cooked ham
$1/2$ tsp caramel syrup
$1^1/_2$ tsps butter
2 tsps ghee for frying ham
1 tsp ghee
2 big pieces of tomatoes
250 gms peas
250 gms beans

Fry onion in butter until light brown, then add boiled rice and salt, then stir it for a few minutes. Fry cooked ham for two minutes. Now fry tomato pieces in 1 tsp ghee with caramel syrup and salt. Cook peas, beans and spinach separately in 6 tsps butter.

How to Arrange Plates for American Chicken

Put cooked rice in the centre of an oval-shaped plate and on it put fried chicken all round, cooked ham, fried tomatoes and peas, beans and spinach. Serve hot at dinner or lunch.

CHICKEN MARYLAND   serves 2

2 chicken breasts
1 level tsp salt
3 green chillies
2 tsps chopped coriander leaves
breadcrumbs for coating
1 beaten egg
3 tsps flour
1 small onion
3 tsps worcestershire sauce
ghee for shallow frying

Beat the chicken breast. Make a paste of all the ingredients, except ghee and breadcrumbs. Dip the chicken breast in it and put on breadcrumbs and flatten it with a knife. Coat both sides with bread-crumbs. Heat ghee, fry the chicken till golden brown. Then pour 3 t ps melted butter over it and all around fried potato fingers

2 or 3 bananas
6 tsps flour
1/2 tsp baking powder
1/4 tsp sugar

1 small egg
4 tsps water
1/4 tsp salt
250 gms potatoes
  (potato fingers)

Beat whites of egg till frothy but not stiff. Make a paste of yolk of egg, flour, salt, sugar, water, baking powder and then in it mix lightly white of egg. Dip 8 pieces of banana and then fry it on medium fire till golden brown. Drain on paper.

BAKED CREAM CHICKEN WITH VEGETABLES *serves 6*

1/2 kg chicken
2 medium size potatoes
3 medium pieces
  cauliflower
3 tsps lemon juice
1/2 tsp white pepper
2 or 2 1/2 cup milk
1/2 onion
craft cheese

1 carrot
225 gms peas
10 level tsps flour
1 green chilli (chopped)
1 tsp cream
salt to taste
5 tsps butter
1/2 tsp chopped coriander

Chop the vegetables, boil them in salted water. Boil chicken with a little salt and water until tender, remove the bones and cut into small pieces.

Fry chopped onion and flour in butter for one minute, add milk and stir it for a few minutes. Add lemon juice, salt, pepper, chopped coriander leaves, green chillies, vegetables and chicken pieces and cook for 5 minutes. Remove from fire, add cream and 1/2 oz grated cheese and mix. Pour into a greased pie dish and sprinkle the rest of grated cheese on top. Bake in moderate oven (350° F) until light brown in colour. Serve it at lunch or dinner.

BAKED CHICKEN (Ukrainian Style) *serves 4*

4 breasts with ribs
  (from two chickens)
1/2 tsp white pepper

1/4 grated cheese
1 level tsp salt
1 egg

1/4 cup flour
1/4 cup water for egg
1 cup curd
ghee for deep drying
breadcrumbs for coating
1/2 cup water for curd

Wash the chicken breast and chop it. Mix salt, pepper and flour together and roll the chicken breast with bone in it. Beat egg with water and in it dip the chicken breast and roll it on breadcrumbs and fry in ghee till golden brown. Arrange the fish on a baking dish and on it pour the curd mixed with water and sprinkle cheese. Bake (350°F) till tender and golden brown.

CHICKEN SANDWICHES   serves 6

12 bread slices
1/8 tsp white pepper
2 tsps mayonnaise sauce
1/4 tsp salt
chicken breast of one chicken
1/2 cup salted butter

Make a paste of mayonnaise sauce, butter, pepper and salt and keep aside. Boil chicken with 1/2 level tsp salt till tender and then chop it. Spread the butter paste on slice and then arrange chopped chicken and cover with other buttered slices. Keep it wrapped in freezing chamber till butter paste is set. Remove the hard crust from the slices and cut into sandwich shape. Decorate with parsley leaves and grated carrot. (Soak the grated carrot in water for one hour.)

CLUB SANDWICHES   serves 4

6 slices of bread
1/4 tsp mustard powder
1 egg omelette
1 tomato
1/2 cup cashewnuts
2 gherkins
ghee for frying
1/4 cup salted butter
1/8 tsp white pepper
1/4 cup cooked ham
1 boiled chicken breast
2 big potatoes
2 preserved onions

Cream the butter and then in it mix mustard powder, chopped gherkins and preserved onion. Brown the bread slices from one side and then cut the hard crusts. Spread butter mixture on unbrowned slices. Fry boiled chicken pieces in ghee for a few minutes. First put ham pieces, tomato slices, fried chicken, omelette and then buttered slice. Press well together. Fasten with 4 toothpicks and cut out into 4 triangles. Put them on a plate and decorate with cashewnuts and potato wafers. Serve at tea.

How to Fry Cashewnuts
Fry cashewnuts in a little hot ghee till light brown. Drain on paper and sprinkle salt on them.

Potato Wafers
Peel and cut potatoes into round and very thin slices. Soak in water for 45 minutes and then dry with clean cloth. Fry in hot ghee till golden brown, drain on paper and sprinkle salt on them.

CHICKEN SHASHLIK *serves 6*

Same recipe as for Pork Shashlik. Omit pork flits and take 2 chicken breasts.

CHICKEN TOAST (French Style) *serves 8*

2 chicken breasts
4 tsps flour
$1/4$ tsp white pepper
9 coriander leaves
8 bread slices
1 firm tomato

2 cups milk
2 tsps lemon juice
$1/2$ tsp worcestershire sauce
5 tsps butter
salt to taste

Boil chicken with $1/2$ tsp salt till tender, remove the bones and chop it. Fry flour in butter till very golden in colour, add milk and cook till a little thick. Remove from fire, mix chicken pieces, white pepper, salt, lemon juice and sauce. Put on buttered toast and decorate with chopped coriander leaves and firm tomato pieces without pulp. Serve at breakfast.

CHICKEN OMELETTE SOUFFLE *serves 2*

2 eggs
1 chicken breast (boiled and chopped)
1 tsp coriander leaves

3 tsps ghee
$1/4$ tsp white pepper
salt to taste
1 green chilli (chopped)

Separate the yolks from whites of eggs. Beat yolks, white pepper and salt. Whip the whites to a stiff froth and fold lightly into the yolk. Mix green chilli, coriander leaves and chopped chicken. Melt ghee in frying pan, pour the egg mixture and stir on the surface until it begins to set. Sprinkle chicken on the omelette. Leave until nicely browned underneath, slip a knife under it and fold first from one side and then from the other towards the centre. Serve at breakfast.

FISH

FISH BAKED WITH NOODLES *serves 6*

$1/2$ kg sole fish
butter

$1 1/4$ cup noodles
$1/2$ cup fresh breadcrumbs, cheese, sauce

Steam the fish, remove the bones and skin and mash it coarsely. Boil noodles in hot salted water until tender, drain. Arrange fish and noodles in layers in a greased dish and then pour cheese sauce. On top sprinkle soft breadcrumbs and put small pieces of butter on it. Bake in moderate oven (350°) until light brown. Serve hot at lunch or dinner.

Cheese Sauce

3 tsps butter
1 tsp salt
$1 1/2$ cups milk
$1/2$ tsp mustard powder

$1 1/2$ tbsps flour
$1/4$ tsp white pepper
6 tsp grated cheese

Melt butter on slow fire, add flour, salt and pepper and stir until slightly golden brown. Remove from fire, add milk and stir. Cook on fire until thick and smooth. Mix grated cheese and mustard powder and cook until cheese is melted. Remove from fire and pour on fish and noodles.

FRIED SOLE FISH *serves 4*

225 gms fish
$1/4$ tsp red chill powder
salt to taste

$1/4$ tsp white pepper
$1/4$ tsp amchoor sauce
$1 1/2$ tsp lemon juice

28 gms flour
breadcrumbs
ghee for frying

2 tsps worcestershire
   sauce
1 or 2 eggs

Remove the bones and skin. Wash and dry fish with cloth. Cut into thin slices and rub red chilli powder or white pepper, lemon juice and worcestershire sauce. Leave the fish in the spices for half an hour. Dredge well with flour, dip in beaten egg and roll on breadcrumbs. Fry the fish in hot ghee until very light brown, lift the fish out of fat and then again fry it until nicely browned. Drain on paper. Serve hot at dinner with potato chips.

FISH CUTLETS   serves 6

250 gms fish
  (sole or singhara)
3 tsps butter
4 tsps flour
2 green chillies (chopped)
breadcrumbs for coating
ghee for deep frying
2 medium sized potatoes (boiled)

$1/2$ cup milk
4 tsps worcestershire
   sauce
2 tsps chopped onion
1 egg
salt to taste
$1/4$ tsp white pepper

Steam the fish, remove bones and skin, then mash it. Fry flour, onion and green chillies in butter till very slightly golden brown. Add milk, cook till thick. Remove from fire, mix fish, grated potato, salt and worcestershire sauce. Make into shape of cutlets (oval shape). Dip into beaten egg mixed with $1/4$ cup of water, coat with breadcrumbs. Deep fry in ghee till golden brown. Serve at tea or at breakfast.

FISH SOUFFLE   serves 8

$1/2$ kg sole fish
$1/4$ tsp white pepper
$1/2$ cup soft bread-
  crumbs
3 egg yolks
2 green chillies

$1/2$ tsp salt
2 tsps lemon juice
$1/2$ onion finely chopped
$1/2$ cup milk
2 egg whites
3 tsps finely chopped
   coriander leaves

Steam the fish, then remove bones and skin. Mash it coarsely and then add salt, pepper, lemon juice, chopped green chillies, onion and coriander leaves. Cook breadcrumbs in milk for a few minutes. Beat egg yolks lightly. Add into fish, breadcrumbs cooked in milk and yolks of egg. Beat whites of egg until stiff. Fold it lightly into fish mixture. Grease the pie dish, pour the fish mixture and bake in moderate oven (350° F) until firm. Serve with Hollandaise sauce.

Hollandaise Sauce

$1/2$ tsp butter   2 egg yolks ($1/2$ cup)
$1/2$ tsp salt   pinch of red chilli powder
1 tbsp lemon juice   1 or 2 tbsps whipped cream

Beat butter until creamy and then beat in egg yolks one at a time. Add lemon juice, salt, red chilli powder. Cook over a pan of hot water until slightly thick. Then mix whipped cream. Serve with fish souffle.

SPAGHETTI WITH MEAT BALLS IN TOMATO SAUCE *serves 6*

225 gms cooked ham $1/2$ cup dry breadcrumbs
$1/4$ cup grated cheese   1 tbsp chopped
$1/4$ tsp white pepper   coriander leaves
1 small chopped onion   1 egg (beaten)
$1/4$ cup milk   4 chopped green chillies
ghee for frying

Mince the cooked ham and then in it add all the ingredients and mix well. Make small balls, dust with flour and fry in ghee until brown.

Tomato Sauce

$3/4$ kg tomatoes   1 tbsp chopped coriander
1 bay leaf   2 tsps sugar
3 chopped green chillies $1^{1}/_{2}$ or 2 level tsps salt
1 tsp worcestershire sauce

Chop tomatoes into small pieces and cook until tender. Strain, then add chopped coriander, green chillies, salt, sugar, bay leaf, worcestershire sauce and fried meat balls. Cook on slow fire for a few minutes.

Spaghetti

200 gms spaghetti	3 tsps butter
1 tsp salt	

Break spaghetti into small pieces. Boil in salted water until tender and drain. Wash with cold water and then fry in 1 oz butter. Put it in a serving plate, then pour sauce and meat balls over it. Sprinkle $1/4$ oz of grated cheese and serve hot at lunch or dinner.

FISH CREAM PEARS serves 4

226 gms fish (without bones and skin)	2 tsps chopped onion
	$1/4$ tsp white pepper
a few coriander leaves	2 tsps butter
6 tsps flour	salt to taste
2 or 3 green chillies	$1/2$ tsp anchovy sauce
4 tsps worcestershire sauce	1 egg
	$1/2$ cup milk
6 tsps cream	dry breadcrumbs for coating
4 tsps thick cream for filling	

Steam the fish till tender. Put on a strainer and then mash coarsely. Fry onion, green chillies and flour in butter for few minutes. Add milk and 6 tsps cream and stir till thick. Remove from fire, mix mashed fish, coriander leaves, pepper and both the sauces. Cool or keep it in the fridge. Shape into pears. Whip 4 tsps cream with fork, and then fill it in chillied fish, dust with crumbs. Dip into beaten egg mixed with 3 tsps of water and then coat with breadcrumbs. Fry in ghee till nicely brown and then decorate with mint leaves and all around put fried potatoes. Serve at lunch, dinner or tea.

FRIED FISH WITH MUSHROOMS
(Thailand Style) serves 6

8 fish slices	6 dried mushrooms (medium)
4 tsps coriander	ghee or fat for deep frying

¾ cup vinegar
¾ cup water
4 tsps chopped spring onion
2 tsps soya sauce

¾ cup flour
2 tsps salt
½ cup sugar
1 tsp ginger powder
3 tsps cornflour

Soak mushrooms in water for 3 hours. Rub ½ tsp salt on the fish. Make a paste of flour, ½ tsp salt and water and in it dip fish and deep fry in ghee till golden brown. Drain on paper.

Drain the mushrooms and chop finely. Boil vinegar with sugar, spring onion, mushrooms, soya sauce, ginger powder and 1 tsp salt, till sugar is dissolved. Mix cornflour in ½ cup water and stir it into vinegar mixture till a little thick. Arrange the fish on a serving dish and on it pour the mushroom mixture and sprinkle coriander leaves on it.

(Indian Mushrooms: soak it for 6 hours and boil till a little tender.)

FISH WITH RICE (Damascus Style)   serves 6

6 fillets of fish
2 tsps lemon juice
½ tsp white pepper
2 cups rice
1 tsp parsley or coriander leaves

½ cup flour
1½ level tsps salt
½ cup butter
¼ cup butter for rice

Wash and dry the fillets and on it rub 1 tsp salt, ¼ tsp white pepper and lemon juice and dust it with flour. Melt butter in frying pan and fry fillets till golden brown. Arrange on serving dish, on it spread rice mixed with tomato pulp and sprinkle coriander leaves.

Rice Preparation
Wash and soak the rice for 15 minutes. Boil it in water till tender. Put it on the strainer, heat the tomato pulp with ½ tsp salt and ¼ tsp pepper and then mix butter and boiled rice and serve.

BAKED FISH (Greek Style)   serves 6

6 fish slices (½" thick)
4 medium sized onions

5 tomatoes
2 garlic flakes (minced)

½ cup butter
½ tsp white pepper
½ cup water
1 tsp salt for fish
3 tsps lemon juice
¼ cup olive oil

Fry garlic flakes with onion slices in olive oil till very slightly golden in colour. Keep aside. Rub ¾ tsp salt and lemon juice on the fish. Melt butter in baking dish and in it arrange fish. Keep a little space between each slice and over and round the fish spread fried onion slices and tomato slices. Sprinkle ¼ tsp salt and on it pour water and bake (375° F) till fish is tender.

FISH FINGERS serves 4

1 or 2 eggs
6 tsps flour
1½ tsps lemon juice
½ tsp anchovy sauce
water to make a paste
350 gms fish
½ tsp China salt (ajino-moto)
½ tsp black pepper
salt to taste

Wash the fish and dry with duster, Sprinkle lemon juice and ½ tsp salt on it. Cut small pieces of fish. Beat eggs, add flour, salt, anchovy sauce, black pepper and China salt. Dip the fish pieces into egg mixture and roll in breadcrumbs and then roll on wooden board to shape into fingers. Deep fry in ghee until brown on all sides. Drain on paper and serve hot with tomato sauce. Serve at tea or cocktail party.

BAKED FISH WITH CHEESE serves 6

½ kg pomfret fish
¼ tsp white pepper
¼ cup flour for dusting
3 tsps lemon juice
1 tsp salt for fish
¼ cup butter

For the Fish
Wash and dry the fish slices. Rub salt, pepper and lemon juice and then dust it with flour. Fry it in butter till tender and slightly brown in colour. Put it on a paper and keep aside.

French Sauce

$2^1/_2$ cups milk	4 tsps flour
1 tsp onion	5 tsps butter
2 tsps cornflour	$1/_4$ tsp white pepper
salt to taste	1 tsp lemon juice
$1/_2$ cup grated cheese (craft or Amul)	

Fry the flour and onion in butter till very slightly brown in colour, add milk and cook till a little thick. Mix cornflour in $1/_4$ cup water and stir it in milk mixture till thick. Mix salt, pepper and lemon juice. Pour a little milk mixture in a pie dish and on it arrange fried fish and pour the rest of milk mixture over it and sprinkle cheese. Bake it in a hot oven (375° F) till cheese is golden brown.

MUTTON

MUTTON CUTLETS   serves 8

$1/_2$ kg keema (minced meat)	1 small onion
6 tsps worcestershire sauce	3 green chillies (chopped)
2 garlic flakes	4 tsps dry breadcrumbs
2 bread slices (soak it in water and squeeze out)	salt to taste
	ghee for deep frying
breadcrumbs for dry coating	1 egg
1 tsp chopped coriander leaves	

Cook keema with chopped onion, garlic and $1^1/_2$ cups, water till tender and dry. Mix bread slices, green chilli, 4 tsps breadcrumbs, salt, worcestershire sauce and coriander leaves. Make oval-shaped cutlets, dip into beaten egg mixed with $1/_4$ cup water and coat with breadcrumbs. Fry till golden brown. Serve at tea or breakfast.

ROASTED MUTTON LEG   serves 6

1 mutton leg	2 level tsps salt
2 tbsps ghee	2 tsps caramel syrup
For decoration: lettuce leaves, 2 beetroots, 2 raddish, 1 carrot and 4 tomatoes	

Fry mutton with salt in ghee until brown. Add caramel syrup and 2 cups water and mix well. Put in pressure cooker and steam until tender, or cook on slow fire in vessel. Remove from ghee and chill. Remove the bones cut into thin and round pieces and decorate with jullienu of raddish, beetroot, carrot and lettuce leaves. Sprinkle vinegar sauce on mutton. Also serve in separate plate lettuce leaves, round pieces of raddish, tomatoes and boiled beet and sprinkle vinegar sauce. Serve at dinner.

Vinegar Sauce

1 tsp mayonnaise sauce
$1/2$ level tsp sugar
$1/4$ tsp salt
$1/4$ level tsp mustard
$1/2$ tsp salad oil
$1/2$ cup vinegar

Make a paste of salad oil, sugar, mustard powder, mayonnaise sauce and salt, then add vinegar and mix well. Strain and sprinkle on salad and cold meat.

MINCED MEAT AND POTATO PEARS serves 8

$1/2$ kg minced meat
4 green chillies
1 egg for dipping
a few coriander leaves
2 garlic flakes
salt to taste
2 tsps ghee
ghee for frying

350 gms potatoes
4 tsps worcestershire sauce
tomato ketchup
1 small onion
1 tsp chopped ginger
$3/4$ tsp white pepper
a few mint leaves
dry breadcrumbs for coating

Boil the potatoes in salted water till tender. Cool and then grate them. Fry chopped onion, chopped green chillies, ginger for few minutes, add minced meat, salt, white pepper and one cup of water and cook till tender and dry. Mix worcestershire sauce, coriander leaves and cool. In it mix grated potatoes. Make into shape of pears, then in it fill tomato ketchup. Dip into beaten egg and coat with breadcrumbs. Fry in hot ghee till nicely brown. Decorate with mint leaves. Serve with potato fingers at lunch or dinner. Without potato fingers serve it at breakfast and tea.

PATE DE FOIE GRAS COCKTAIL
(French Style)
serves 6

115 gms liver	2 small onions
2 bay leaves	2 green chillies
1/2 tsp salt	2 tsps worcestershire sauce
3 tsps butter	1 1/2 tbsps ghee
1/2 level tsp mustard powder	1/2 tsp black pepper

Fry onion slices and bay leaves until light brown, then add big pieces of liver, chopped green chillies, salt, pepper, mustard powder and worcestershire sauce and fry for a few minutes on slow fire stirring frequently, until dry. Cool, then grind finely with the same ghee. Heat butter and mix into ground liver and put in small loaf tin and chill until firm. Cut into slices. Put ice in the centre of the plate and on it put liver slices and decorate with jullienne of carrot, lettuce leave and beatroot. Serve at cocktail party.

BRAIN CUTLETS
serves 6

3 brains of lamb	2 green chillies
1 onion	2 tbsps flour
1/4 tsp mustard powder	salt to taste
1/2 tsp white pepper	1 egg
3 tsps worcestershire sauce	1 1/2 cups dry breadcrumbs
ghee for deep frying	for coating

Boil brains in salted water for a few minutes. Cool and then cut into two pieces. Chop onion, green chillies finely. Rub all the ingredients on brain except egg and breadcrumbs. First dip brains in beaten eggs and then roll in breadcrumbs. Fry in hot ghee until light brown and then drain on paper. Serve hot with potato chips at lunch or dinner.

MEAT PIE
serves 6

1/2 kg minced meat	1/3 cup butter
1 oz cream	6 tsps flour
3 eggs	1 tsp chopped coriander
salt to taste	leaves

¼ cup grated cheese
½ tsp white pepper
¼ tsp mustard powder
2 fresh green chillies
small onion

Fry onion in half the butter until light brown, add minced meat, white pepper, mustard powder, chopped coriander leaves and green chillies and cook until dry. Remove from fire and cool. Cream the butter and mix yolks, cream, and 3 tsps flour and heat. Beat egg whites until stiff, then fold in the remaining flour and grated cheese. Now fold into the yolk mixture lightly. Pour half of the mixture into a greased pie fish and then spread cooked minced meat. Now spread the remaining half of the egg mixture on top. Bake it in 350°F until set and lightly browned on the top. Serve hot at lunch or dinner with raddish cream.

MUTTON PIZZA *serves 6*

The same recipe as for Tomato and Cheese Pizza. Omit the onion slices and cheese. Arrange cooked minced meat mixed with tomato pulp. Sprinkle coriander on it and bake.

Filling
250 gms minced meat
salt to taste
¼ tsp white pepper
a few coriander leaves

Cook minced meat with salt, pepper and I cup water till tender and dry, mix it in tomato filling of tomato and cheese pizza.

ASHAK (Afghanistan Style)

1 cup flour
1 egg
½ tsp salt

Sift flour and salt and knead with egg till dough is smooth; if a little stiff mix a little water and knead it. Keep it covered for 5 minutes. Pull the dough lightly on a floured wooden board as thin as possible. Cut into round shapes with fancy round cutter. Coat the edges with a little beaten egg and fill with the leek or spring onion stuffing.

Stuffing (with white and green part)
1½ tsps salt   1 chopped green chilli
250 gms leek (¼ lb) or
    250 gms spring onion

Chop the leak or spring onion and rub salt till it leaves its water. Mix chopped green chilli, squeeze out its water till dry. Fill it in the fancy round pieces of dough and fold it. Steam till it becomes a little soft and put it on strainer.

For Decoration
1 cup sour curd   1½ tsps dry mint leaves
¼ tsp salt   1 crushed garlic flake

Put the curd in muslin cloth and hang till dry. Mix salt and garlic. Spread a little curd on a serving dish, on it put steamed Ashak and again spread curd over it and sprinkle crushed dry mint leaves and decorate with cooked minced meat.

Minced Meat of Lamb
250 gms minced meat   2 big tomatoes
2 medium onions   ½ tsp red chilli powder
few coriander leaves   ¼ cup ghee
salt to taste

Filling
Fry onion slices till golden brown, add chopped tomatoes and stir till well mixed. Then in it cook minced meat with salt and red chilli powder and 1½ cups water till tender and dry, spread over the curd and sprinkle coriander over it.

STUFFED CAPSICUMS (Arabic Style)

10 capsicums medium   250 gms minced (lamb)
½ cup tomato ketchup   1 onion (sliced)
3 medium tomatoes   2 tsps parsley leaves or
1 tsp coriander leaves   ¼ tsp red chilli powder
salt to taste   ¼ cup ghee
2 green chillies chopped   ½ cup boiled and
½ cup water   drained rice

Fry onion slices in ghee till golden brown, mix peeled and chopped tomatoes and fry till dry. Mix minced meat, green chillies and stir till dry. Add 1 cup water and cook till tender and water is evaporated. Mix boiled rice, chopped coriander leaves and salt. Keep aside.

Cut one inch piece of the tops of each capsicum and scoop out the seeds carefully and stuff with filling. Arrange them in a baking dish and on them pour tomato ketchup mixed with $1/2$ cup water and chilli powder. Bake (350°F) over a pan of water till tender. Garnish with coriander leaves and serve.

LIVER TOAST
serves 4

250 gms liver
salt to taste
$1^{1}/_{2}$ tsps mustard powder
1 tsp ghee
6 tsps worcestershire sauce
1 big onion
2 or 3 green chillies
$1/2$ tsp black pepper
2 tsps caramel syrup
8 slices bread
ghee for frying bread slices

Heat ghee, add chopped onion, green chillies and washed small pieces of liver, salt, mustard powder, black pepper, caramel syrup and worcestershire sauce and cook till tender and a little dry. Fry bread slices in ghee till golden in colour and put cooked liver mixture on the toast. Serve hot at breakfast.

SCRAMBLED EGGS WITH HAM ON TOAST
serves 2

3 tsps butter
$1/4$ cup chopped cooked ham
salt to taste
salted butter for toast
$1/2$ onion
4 eggs
2 green chillies
12 tsps cream
1 small tomato without pulp
4 bread slices

Chop onion, tomato and green chillies finely. Put eggs, chopped ham, cream and salt in bowl and beat until light, melt butter in small frying pan, then add egg mixture and stir until thick. Then put on buttered toast and serve at breakfast.

HAM OMELETTE SOUFFLE *serves 2*

Take ¼ cup chopped cooked ham.
See the recipe for Chicken Omelette Souffle. Omit chicken breast.

PORK

GRILLED PORK CHOPS *serves 4*

4 or 5 pork chops
½ tsp salad oil
1 tsp white pepper
salt to taste
3 tsps worcestershire sauce
½ kg small potatoes
  (boiled in salted water
  and then fried)
3 tsps salad oil
½ tsp mustard powder
3 small tomatoes
2 tsps caramel syrup
6 tsps ghee or 6 tsps salad
  oil for shallow frying

Beat chops with rolling pin till flat. Make a paste of mustard powder, white pepper, salad oil, salt, worcestershire sauce and rub it on chops and keep for 15 minutes. Then fry chops in ghee or salad oil for shallow frying (pork leaves its ghee) till golden brown and tender. Now mix caramel syrup. Remove the chops from the ghee or salad oil and in it fry whole tomatoes (cut from both sides), fry the boiled potatoes in chops fat. Put the chops on an oval shaped dish and then all around put fried tomatoes and potatoes. Serve at lunch or dinner.

STUFFED EGGS *serves 6*

5 or 6 full boiled eggs
1 tsp chopped coriander
  leaves
3 tsps worcestershire sauce
¼ tsp salt
breadcrumbs for coating
1 cup cooked ham
  (chopped)
2 or 3 green chillies
¼ or ½ cup milk
1 small beaten egg
ghee for frying

Cut the eggs lengthwise into half. Remove the yolks of eggs and mash them. Mix chopped cooked ham, green chillies, coriander leaves, worcestershire sauce, mashed yolks of eggs and milk. Fill the egg cases with the mixture and shape into eggs. Dip into beaten egg and coat it with breadcrumbs, with 3 tsps water. Fry in hot ghee till golden brown. Drain on paper. Serve hot at cocktail parties, at tea or breakfast.

PORK SHASHLIK   serves 5

2 pork flits or undercuts
4 tomatoes slices
  (without pulp)
1 onion
3 tbsps curd
3 tsps salad oil

3 big onion slices
4 green chillies
1 tsp turmeric
4 small slices of fresh
  ginger
salt to taste

Chop onion, ginger, and green chillies very finely. Mix into curd, turmeric, salad oil, salt, chopped onion, ginger and green chillies and then put in big pork pieces and let it remain for one hour. First put onion slices on the iron rod and then tomato slices and pork pieces and pack it tightly. By this process finish all the meat and vegetable pieces on 2 or 3 rods. Put rods on medium fire and turn frequently until mixture is dry or grill and pour 3 tbsps salad oil little by little on pork pieces until light brown. Serve hot with round onion and tomato slices. Serve at tea or cocktail party.

HAM AND PINEAPPLE LOAF

1 cup cooked ham
4 tsps brown sugar
1 green chilli
$1/4$ tsp mustard powder
no salt (as ham is salted)
$1/4$ cup pineapple juice
1 egg

3 tsps butter
1 tsp coriander leaves
$1/2$ tsp ground ginger
pineapple and cherry for
  decoration
$1/2$ cup fresh breadcrumbs
$1/4$ tsp red chilli powder

Melt butter in loaf tin and then sprinkle brown sugar over it. Decorate pineapple pieces with cherry on top of sugar. Mix chopped ham, finely chopped onion, red chilli powder, fresh breadcrumbs, pineapple juice, ground ginger, coriander leaves, mustard powder and slightly beaten egg together. Put the ham mixture on the top of pineapple pieces with cherry. Bake in moderate oven for about 25 to 30 minutes. Turn upside down on a plate and keep for 10 minutes so that brown sugar's syrup may not trickle down. Serve hot at lunch or dinner.

FRIED PORK CHOPS   serves 4

4 pork chops
1 small raw papaya
4 tsps salad oil
ghee for shallow frying
$1/2$ level tsp mustard powder
8 tsps worcestershire sauce
2 level tsps salt
$1/2$ tsp white pepper

Peel the papaya and then grind finely and take out its juice. Make a paste with mustard powder, salad oil, worcestershire sauce, white pepper, and salt. Beat the chops, then soak in the paste for half an hour. Heat ghee in frying pan, put chops with 1 cup water and cook till dry and fry on slow fire until golden brown. Serve with grilled tomatoes.

Grilled Tomatoes
350 gms tomatoes
salt to taste
1 or $1/2$ tbsp ghee
6 tsps caramel syrup
3 tsps worcestershire sauce

Cut the thin slices from both ends of tomatoes. Heat ghee and fry with caramel syrup, salt and sauce until half cooked, serve with fried pork chops.

EGG NUN STYLE   serves 6

6 hard boiled eggs
$1 1/2$ tsps craft cheese
$1/2$ level tsp white pepper
$1 1/2$ tsps flour
1 egg
1 tsp coriander leaves (chopped)
225 gms cooked ham
$1/4$ tsp salt
3 green chillies (finely chopped)
$1 1/2$ cups dry breadcrumbs

Cut hard boiled eggs lengthwise and remove the yolks. Chop ham very finely. In yolks mix cooked ham, cheese, salt, pepper, green chillies and coriander leaves. Fill egg whites with yolk mixture and shape so that each half looks like a whole egg. Dust with flour, dip into beaten egg mixed with two tsps water, coat with dry breadcrumbs, and deep dry in ghee till golden brown. Serve hot at tea or breakfast.

SAUSAGES WITH SPAGHETTI serves 6

- 1/2 kg cocktail sausages (small size)
- 1/4 level tsp white pepper
- 1/4 level tsp red chill powder
- 1 tsp salt for boiling spaghetti
- 3 tsps butter for spaghetti
- 1 tsp salt
- 1/2 kg tomato
- 1 tsp worcestershire sauce
- 1 tsp sugar (for tomato)
- 226 gms spaghetti

Break the spaghetti into medium pieces. Boil water with salt and in it cook spaghetti till it becomes tender. Put on a strainer. Wash with water. Fry in butter with salt to taste and white pepper. Remove from fire and keep it aside. Prick the sausages with a toothpick or fine needle (knitting) and cook with 1/2 cup of water, till the water is evaporated. Then fry them in their own fat till golden brown. Remove from the fat and keep aside. Cook some pieces of tomatoes till tender and then strain. Cook tomato pulp with sugar, salt, worcestershire sauce and red chilli powder till it boils. Add fried sausages, spaghetti and cook for one or two minutes. Put in serving dish, garnish with coriander leaves. Serve at lunch or dinner.

FRIED SAUSAGES (Italian Style) serves 6

- 1/2 kg cocktail sausages
- 5 tsps butter
- 1/4 tsp white pepper
- 1/2 onion
- 2 tsps chopped coriander leaves
- salt to taste
- 1/2 kg peas or beans
- salt to taste (for peas)
- 350 gms tomatoes
- 2 cloves
- 1 bayleaf
- 2 tsps sugar
- 1/4 tsp red chilli powder

Boil peas or beans until tender. Fry in butter with salt and pepper to taste.

HAM SANDWICHES   serves 8

The same recipe as for chicken. Omit chicken and take 6 thin slices of cooked ham and do not chop them, but arrange in flat slices.

MAGIC SAUSAGE ROLLS   serves 10

$1/2$ kg potatoes
1 level tsp salt
1 beaten egg
ghee for frying

$1/4$ tsp white pepper
dry breadcrumbs for coating
250 gms cocktail sausages

Boil the potatoes with $1/2$ tsp salt till tender. Cool, peel and grate, mix salt and pepper and keep it aside. Now prick the sausages with fork and cook with 1 cup water till dry and then fry them in their own fat. Fill in grated potato and make oblong balls. Dip into beaten egg mixed with 3 tsps water and roll in breadcrumbs. Fry in hot ghee till golden brown. Serve at tea.

PUDDINGS AND ICE CREAMS

PUDDINGS
APPLE TART
serves 6

1 cup flour (pressed)
6 tsps butter
$1/2$ tsp baking powder
$1/2$ cup water
2 cloves

4 tsps castor sugar
1 egg yolk
250 gms apples
2 or $2^{1}/_{2}$ tbsps sugar

Cream the butter and sugar. Add egg and beat it nicely. Sift flour, baking powder. Put the mixture on wooden board and mix sifted flour and baking powder lightly. Roll it $1/4$" thick and prick it and arrange it in ungreased ring mould. Press the edges and bake in moderate oven (350° F) till light brown.

Peel and cut small pieces of apples, cook on slow fire with water till tender. Add sugar, cloves and stir till dry. Cool a little and fill in the baked tart.

Meringue
3 whites of eggs   8 tsps sugar

Beat egg whites till stiff. Beat it gradually with sugar. Spread half the mixture over the cooked apples and the rest put in piping paper and decorate the tart with it. Bake the tart again in moderate oven till meringue is crisp and golden brown. Serve warm with cream.

BREAD PUDDING (Italian Style)
serves 8

12 bread slices
$1/4$ tsp raisins

2 cups milk
$1/2$ cup cream

2 tsp finely chopped lemon peel
2 eggs
1 tsp vanilla essence
1/4 cup peeled almonds

5 tsps butter
1/4 castor sugar
1 egg yolk
1 1/2 tbsps jam

Add cream, eggs and yolk, castor sugar and vanilla essence into milk and mix well. Fill a greased loaf tin with thin slices of buttered bread and on each layer spread jam lightly and sprinkle raisins and lemon peels. Then on it pour the milk mixture and keep it for 35 minutes. Sprinkle coarsely chopped almonds on the pudding. Bake for about 35 or 45 minutes in a hot oven (375°F) or until nicely browned on the top. Cool and then cut into slices and serve with cream custard separately.

Cream Custard

3 cups milk
1/2 cup sugar
2 tbsps cornflour

1/2 cup cream
1 egg
1/2 tsp vanilla essence

Boil milk with sugar. Beat egg yolks with cornflour and then mix into boiling milk and stir it on low heat until the mixture is thick. Cool, then add cream and vanilla essence and serve with bread pudding.

BANANA TRIFLE PUDDING   serves 6

2 eggs
1/2 cup flour
250 gms cream
cherry jam
1/3 cup castor sugar

1/3 cup sugar
3 or 4 bananas
2 tbsps jam
1/2 cup cherry

Beat the eggs and sugar over the pan of hot water until frothy. Mix sifted flour lightly. Grease the round mould and then dust with flour. Pour the mixture in it and bake in hot moderate oven. Insert wooden pick into the cake, if it comes out smoothly then it is ready. Cut the sponge cake into two layers and then sandwich it with jam. Whip the cream with castor sugar. Cut long slices of cake and put in serving dish and on it put round pieces of bananas and then spread whipped cream. Repeat the process until all the cake pieces, bananas and cream have been used up. Then decorate the top of the pudding with the remaining whipped thick cream and cherry.

BANANA PUDDING (Swedish Style)   serves 6

$1/2$ cup butter   sugar ($3/4$ cup)
2 eggs   flour (1 cup)
$1/4$ tsp salt   1 tsp baking powder
3 bananas   6 tsps lemon juice
$1/2$ cup dark brown sugar   4 tsps grated coconut

Beat the butter and sugar till fluffy, then beat the eggs one by one and finally mix sifted flour, salt and baking powder together. Preheat oven to 350° F. Grease the square mould with ghee and then dust it with flour. Spread the mixture evenly and on it, arrange long slices of banana and sprinkle lemon juice, brown sugar and coconut. Bake it for about 25 to 30 minutes until wood pick comes out smoothly. Remove from the oven. Unmould on serving dish and then serve it with lightly whipped cream. (1 cup cream and 2 tsps castor sugar.)

BAKED COCONUT CUSTARD   serves 8

2 cups milk   2 cups dried grated coconut
4 eggs

Boil milk with coconut and keep it covered till cold. Take out the milk from the coconut, strain it and discard the pulp. Beat eggs and sugar over a pan of hot water till frothy, then mix coconut milk gradually till well mixed. Put it in 8 individual buttered custard cups and cover with wax paper. Bake over a pan of hot water till custard is set. Sprinkle pink coloured coconut on each cup (mix 1 drop red colour in $1/4$ cup coconut). Serve cold.

CARAMEL CUSTARD   serves 6

3 big eggs   2 cups milk
$1/4$ cup water $1/4$ cup sugar for caramel
$1/3$ tsp vanilla essence $1/3$ cup sugar

Melt ¼ cup sugar in steaming mould till brown in colour, then grease the sides of mould with caramel syrup. Beat eggs, sugar, milk and essence and pour mixture over the caramel. Steam it very gently for about 45 minutes or until the mixture is just firm. Cool it and keep it for one hour and turn it on the dish. Serve at lunch or dinner.

COLD CHOCOLATE CREAM PUDDING   serves 6

3 tsps gelatine
4 egg yolks
¼ tsp salt
⅓ cup crushed chocolate
1 tsp vanilla essence
¼ cup milk
¾ cup sugar
2 cups milk
1½ cups cream
cherries for decoration

Soak gelatine in ¼ cup of milk. Boil rest of milk with chocolate until well dissolved. Beat yolks, sugar and salt and in it mix chocolate milk. Cook over a pan of hot water until mixture boils. Add soaked gelatine and stir until well dissolved. Chill it. When chocolate mixture is half set, beat it and fold in 1 cup of whipped cream and vanilla essence. Pour into greased jelly mould and again chill for 2 hours until set. Turn it on plate and decorate with cherry and cream. (Grease the jelly mould with salad oil.)

CHOCOLATE BREAD PUDDING   serves 6

1 cup milk
4 cherries
5 tsps melted butter
2 eggs
¼ cup raisins
2 cups of fresh bread-crumbs
⅓ cup sugar
⅛ tsp salt
2 tsps cocoa

Vanilla essence or ½ tsp of cinnamom powder

Boil the milk, remove from fire, pour over fresh breadcrumbs and cool, and in it mix melted butter, sugar, cocoa, salt, slightly beaten egg yolks, raisins, cinnamon powder or vanilla essence with wire beater. Pour into buttered pie-dish and set on pan of hot water (2" deep). Bake in moderate oven (350° F) for about one hour till wooden pick inserted in the pudding comes out clean. Decorate the pudding with meringue. Serve hot with lightly whipped cream.

Meringue
2 whites of eggs $1/4$ cup sugar
2 tsp cocoa

Whip the whites of egg till stiff. Mix sugar (keep 2 tsps for sprinkling on the meringue) and cocoa. Put the stiff whites over the baked pudding and sprinkle small pieces of cherries and 2 tsps sugar and bake for five minutes till crisp.

COLD CHOCOLATE PUDDING
(Italian Style) serves 4

$1/2$ cup crushed cooking chocolate
$1/2$ cup milk
$1/8$ tsp salt
2 eggs

$1/2$ tsp vanilla essence
$1/3$ cup sugar
$1/4$ cup water
1 tsp full gelatine
$1/2$ cup cream

Soak gelatine in $1/4$ cup water. Melt chocolate over a pan of water on fire. Mix sugar, salt and milk and stir till sugar is dissolved. Remove from the fire, in it beat yolks of egg one by one and stir it over a pan of water on the fire till a little thick. Cool, fold in stiff egg whites, essence and whipped cream. Line the mould with wax paper; pour chocolate mixture and keep in freezing chamber till firm.

CUSTARD PIE   serves 6

1 cup flour
6 tsps chilled butter
1 beaten egg
2 tsps milk

4 tsps castor sugar
$1/2$ tsp vanilla essence
1 tsp baking powder

Sift flour, baking powder and castor sugar. Rub the chilled butter with fingertips. Mix beaten egg and vanilla essence (if big take half, if small take one), roll it $1/4$" thick into a round shape. Put the ring on the back of the tray, line it with the dough and then fill it with the custard.

Custard
$1/2$ cup sugar
$1/4$ tsp vanilla essence

$3/4$ cup milk
2 big eggs

Beat all the ingredients together with an egg beater for one or two minutes. Pour the mixture in the ring and bake it immediately till it is golden brown and custard is set. Remove the ring from the top and then again bake it till the sides are golden brown. Remove from the oven, cool and then serve at lunch or dinner.

COLD ORANGE PUDDING serves 6

2 tsps gelatine
4 eggs
1/4 tsp salt
1/2 cup orange juice
3/4 tsp cream
1/4 cup cold water
3/4 cup sugar
2 tbsps lemon juice
4 drops of orange essence
1/4 tsp orange colour

Soak gelatine in cold water. Beat egg yolks, salt, lemon, juice, orange juice and 1/2 cup of sugar and cook over the pan of hot water until thick. Add soaked gelatine and stir until dissolved. Remove from fire and cool. Beat white of egg until stiff, then add gradually remaining sugar and orange essence. Mix lightly into yolk mixture. Pour in pie dish. Chill until firm. Decorate with whipped cream.

CHRISTMAS PUDDING serves 8

1 cup heaped fresh breadcrumbs
1 level tsps instant coffee
1/4 tsp soda bicarbonate
2 eggs
1/2 tsp ground cinnamon
1/4 tsp ground cloves
1/2 cup chopped pitted dates
1/4 tsp salt
1/2 cup raisins
1/4 cup butter
2 tsps caramel syrup
1 tsp baking powder
1/4 cup rum
1/2 tsp ground nutmeg
1/2 cup chopped sultana without seeds
1/4 cup peels

Cream the butter with sugar and in it beat eggs. Mix baking powder, soda bicarbonate, all the spices, salt, chopped dry fruit, fresh breadcrumbs, rum, caramel syrup coffee. Grease the steaming mould with butter. Put the mixture in it not more than 3/4 full. Steam it for about 2 hours till set and a little firm. Serve it hot with 1 cup whipped cream.

(This pudding can be kept 3 weeks. Just before serving heat it in the same steaming mould in which pudding is steamed.)

EMBASSY SPECIAL PUDDING serves 6

1 cup cream
$1/2$ tsp vanilla essence
1 tsp gelatine
2 or 3 tbsps water
$1/4$ cup pistachio

$1/4$ tsp salt
$1/2$ cup castor sugar
2 drops of yellow colour
$3/4$ cup of chopped pineapple

Whip cream with castor sugar, vanilla essence, yellow colour and salt. Soak gelatine in one tbsp of water and dissolve over a pan of hot water and mix it into cream. Fold chopped fruit and whole pistachio into whipped cream. Put it into round moulds and freeze till set.

Sponge Cake
2 eggs
$1/3$ cup sugar

$1/2$ tsp. vanilla essence
$1/2$ cup flour

Beat eggs and sugar over a pan of hot water until frothy. Mix or fold flour lightly into egg mixture. Then mix essence, bake in moderate oven (350° F) till wooden pick comes out smooth. Cool it. Cut one layer and fill the frozen mixture and decorate the top with whipped cream.

FRUIT PUDDING WITH CUSTARD serves 6

2 eggs
$1/2$ cup flour

$1/3$ cup sugar
$1/4$ tsp vanilla essence

Beat egg and sugar over a pan of hot water till it becomes frothy. Mix sifted flour lightly and then mix vanilla essence. Grease the heart-shaped mould with ghee and then dust with flour. Pour the mixture in it and then bake it in moderate oven till wooden pick comes out smoothly. Cool on the wire rack covered with cloth.

Custard
3 cups milk
$1/2$ tsp vanilla essence
$1/8$ tsp yellow colour

$3/4$ cup sugar
1 big egg
2 tsps cornflour

1 apple (very small pieces)
1 orange (remove the peels)
2 bananas (cut into round pieces)

Boil 2 cups of milk with sugar, make a paste of egg, cornflour and 1 cup of milk. Now stir it into boiling milk till it is a little thick or coats on the back of the spoon. Remove from the fire and stir it continuously till no lumps are formed. Mix essence and colour. Arrange the fruit on a serving dish, on it pour half the custard and then put the cake over it and pour the remaining custard on the top.

For Decoration
1 cup cream
$1/3$ tsp vanilla essence
4 tsps icing sugar
$1/4$ tsp yellow colour

Beat the cream till thick but not very thick. Then add yellow colour, do not mix it. Decorate it, using a medium nozzle.

(If the colour of the custard is not good then mix one drop of yellow and one drop of orange colour, otherwise there is no need.)

FRUIT GATEUX PUDDING
(French Style)   serves 6

2 eggs
$1/2$ cup flour
2 tbsps water
$1/4$ tsp raspberry red colour
2 slices of pineapple
$1/3$ cup sugar
$1/2$ tsp strawberry essence
2 cups cream
2 apples
$1/3$ cup castor sugar

Beat eggs, sugar and water over a pan of hot water until frothy. Add essence and colour and mix well. Fold sifted flour lightly. Grease the mould and then dust with flour. Pour the mixture in it and then bake it in moderate oven (350° F) until wooden pick comes out smoothly. Cool and then cut into two layers. Whip cream with sugar, $1/4$ tsp essence and red colour. Keep half the cream for decoration and to the remaining portion of cream mix chopped fruit. Spread fruit and cream on the layers of cake and then decorate the top with cream and cherry. Serve at lunch or dinner.

HOT PEACHES PUDDING   serves 8

1/2 cup sugar
2 eggs (big)
1/2 tin of peaches
1/2 level cup thick
    brown sugar
1/2 cup flour
1/4 tsp lemon essence
cherry for decoration
1/4 cup butter
1 tsp caramel syrup for brown sugar

Beat eggs and sugar over a pan of hot water with egg beater till it becomes frothy. Add sifted flour and mix well and add lemon essence. Melt the butter in a heart-shaped mould and in it sprinkle brown sugar. Decorate with peaches (keep the peaches in the mould with half-cut cherry, filled in the hollow side). Cover the peaches with the egg mixture. Bake in moderate oven till wooden pick comes out smoothly. Unmould on the dish and then keep for five minutes. Do not remove the mould for five minutes, otherwise syrup will trickle down. Serve it lukewarn with lightly whipped cream (3/4 cup of cream) in a separate bowl.

HOT SOUFFLE   serves 8

6 tsps butter
1/4 tsp salt
3 eggs
1 tsp cream of tartar
1/3 cup cashewnuts
1 cup cream
1 1/2 cup flour
1 cup milk
1/2 tsp vanilla essence
3/4 cup sugar
5 tsps icing sugar
1/4 tsp vanilla essence for cream

Melt butter and add flour, milk and salt and stir on fire till thick and smooth. Beat egg yolks and sugar till frothy. Mix flour mixture into yolk mixture with vanilla essence. Beat egg white and cream of tartar till stiff, mix lightly into yolk and flour mixture. Pour into greased pie dish, sprinkle cashewnuts and bake it over a pan of hot water (350° F) till it is puffed up, golden brown and wooden pick comes out smoothly. Remove from the oven, then serve it hot with lightly whipped cream mixed with ¼ tsp vanilla essence and icing sugar. Serve at lunch or dinner. (If the milk mixture becomes thick after cooking add little more milk and make it smooth mixture.)

LEMON PUDDING   serves 6

1 cup sugar   1 cup milk
2 big eggs   5 tsps lemon juice
1 tsp grated lemon rind   ¼ cup flour
¼ tsp salt   ¾ cup cream

Beat yolks, sugar and milk and in it mix sifted flour, salt, lemon rind and lemon juice. Beat whites of egg till stiff and fold it into milk mixture, put it in greased glass casserole dish. Bake over a pan of hot water (350 F) till set and golden in colour. Serve it hot with whipped cream.

ICEBERG or FLOATING PUDDING   serves 8

3 eggs (small 5)   2 tsps cornflour
¾ cup sugar   1½ level tsps gelatine
⅓ cup castor sugar   1 tbsp hot water
3½ cups milk   ¾ cup cream
½ tsp vanilla essence   1 cup grapes
1 or 2 bananas   1 tsp dry grated coconut
4 cherries   a few drops of red colour

Beat the egg yolks and sugar with wooden spoon and mix into boiled and cooled milk. Cook over a pan of hot water on slow fire, stirring constantly until it coats the spoon. Remove from the fire and stir for about five minutes. Cool and then mix lightly whipped cream and fruit and pour it into icecream cups. Beat egg whites until stiff, mix vanilla essence and gelatine dissolved in hot water drop by drop and beat it. Now fold castor sugar gradually. Drop the meringue on the custard and decorate with chopped cherry and coloured coconut and again chill it till meringue is set. Serve it at lunch or dinner.

MAGIC BREAD PUDDING   serves 8

1/2 tin condensed milk	1 1/2 cups hot water
1 1/2 cups (heaped) fresh breadcrumbs	1 cup cream
	2 eggs
3 tsps water	1/4 tsp salt
1 tsp salt	1 tsp grated lemon rind
4 tsps raisins	

Mix condensed milk, water, lemon rind and butter together. Then mix crumbs, salt and beaten eggs and keep it till cold. Beat it with a wooden spoon till smooth, mix raisins. Pour it into buttered pie dish and bake it for 45 minutes (in 350° F) till set and golden brown in colour. Serve with whipped cream.

MERINGUE LEMON PIE   serves 6

6 tsps butter	4 tsps castor sugar
1 egg	3/4 cup flour
1/2 tsp baking powder	

For the Pie

Cream butter and sugar together. Add egg and beat it nicely. Then add baking powder and mix it. Put this mixture on a wooden board and mix sifted flour lightly. In summer keep it for five minutes in cool place. Roll it 1/4" thick and fill it in ungreased pie dish and bake in moderate oven. When it is light brown in colour, take it out and cool it. Fill lemon custard in it and pile meringue over the custard and bake in moderate oven for five minutes till crisp and light brown in colour.

Filling—Lemon Custard

3 tsp butter	1/2 cup sugar
1 egg yolk	6 tsps juice of 2 lemons
rind of 2 lemons	3 tsps cornflour
3/4 cup water	3/4 cup milk
few drops of yellow colour	

Put sugar, yolks, cornflour, lemon rind, lemon juice in a small bowl and beat it with a wooden spoon till smooth. Boil the milk with water and butter and keep on fire for 2 minutes. Put the above mixture in the boiling milk and beat it vigorously with a wire beater till it becomes thick. Add yellow colour and mix it. Cool and fill it in the pie dish. Pile the meringue over the lemon custard and sprinkle two tsps castor sugar on it. Bake in moderate oven for 10 minutes, till crisp and golden brown.

Meringue

2 whites of egg   6 tsps sugar
$1/8$ tsp cream of tartar

Beat white of eggs with $1/2$ tsp cream of tartar till stiff. Beat in gradually 1 oz sugar. (Keep 2 tsps of sugar for sprinkling over the meringue.) Continue beating hard till meringue is stiff.

ORANGE SOUFFLE   serves 6

3 big eggs $1/2$ cup of sugar
3 tsps lemon juice $1/2$ cup of orange juice
$1/4$ tsp salt (level) $1/4$ tsp orange colour
$1/2$ tsp orange crush   2 tsps of gelatine
  essence $1/4$ cup of water for
cherry for decoration   soaking the gelatine
$3/4$ cup of cream for decoration

Beat sugar, lemon juice, orange juice (mixed with salt) and yolks of eggs with a wooden spoon. Cook over a pan of hot water till the sugar is dissolved. Add soaked gelatine and stir it till the gelatine is dissolved. Remove from the fire, cool it over the pan of water. Mix orange crush and orange colour. Then beat whites of egg till stiff. Mix it well into the yolk mixture Line the heart-shape mould with a wax paper or grease with salad oil. Then pour the mixture in it. Keep it in the fridge till is set. Then unmould it on the cold plate and decorate it.

Now beat the cream with egg beater till it is little thick. Add $1/4$ tsp colour (orange) but do not mix it. Then decorate the pudding with it and add cherry. (This pudding is served just like ice cream.)

ORANGE BASKET PUDDING serves 12

12 oranges
2 cups water
$1/2$ level tsp salt
orange and red colour
7 or 8 tsps gelatine
$1/2$ tsp orange essence

3 cups orange juice
1 cup sugar
1 cup water for soaking gelatine
1 cup cream
cherry and pistachio for decoration

Make a syrup of sugar and water. Add soaked gelatine and stir it until dissolved. Remove from fire, add orange juice. Strain it and mix orange essence. Divide the liquid into half, then add orange and red colour separately. Put into jelly moulds and chill. Fill the orange basket with jelly and decorate with cream, cherry and pistaschio. Serve at lunch or dinner.

How to Make Orange Basket

The rind of each orange must be shaped in the form of a cup with a narrow handle across the top. Remove half the rind of each orange except the part which forms the handle and then scoop out the pulp and take out the juice and mix salt. (Whip cream with one tbsp castor sugar.)

PEACH BERDOER serves 8

short bread
6 tsps sugar
1 heaped cup flour
$1 1/2$ tsps baking powder

9 tsps butter
3 tbsps milk
1 egg yolk

Cream the butter and sugar until fluffy, add yolk and beat it, add in it milk. Sift flour and baking powder. Put egg mixture on wooden board and mix sifted flour and baking powder. Roll it $1/8$ thick and spread it in ring mould and press it. Bake in moderate oven (350°) until light brown.

Filling—Thick Custard

5 tsps flour
7 tsps sugar
2 cups milk
A few drops of raspberry essence

1 egg yolk
4 tbsps water
8 tsps cream

Mix all the above except essence and cream and cook until quite thick. Cool and strain, then add cream and essence.

Filling in the Baked Short Bread

2 tbsps jam
3 whites of egg
Medium slices of peaches
7 tsps sugar

Spread jam on the bottom of baked short bread and then put half the thick custard on it. Cover the custard with the slices of peaches and spread the rest of the thick custard. Beat whites of egg until stiff and then add sugar gradually and beat it. Spread it on the thick custard and then decorate the top with it. Bake in moderate oven (315^0) until light brown. Serve cold with lightly whipped cream.

STEAMED FRUIT CUSTARD   serves 8

3 cups milk
$1/3$ tsp vanilla essence
10 tsps sugar
$1/3$ tin of cocktail fruit or apples and papayas (cut into small pieces but not very small)
4 small eggs (or 3 big)
2 drops of yellow colour (if the colour is not good)
$1 1/2$ tsp butter

Cook the milk till it reduces to $2 1/2$ or $2 1/4$ cup of milk and cool. In it mix yolks of egg, sugar, vanilla essence, yellow colour and beat with an egg beater for a minute or two. Beat the whites of egg till it is frothy (not stiff). Then mix it into the mixture (the mixture will be quite liquidish).

In the steaming mould melt $1/2$ oz butter. Then pour the mixture in the mould and steam it. In the water put 3 tsps vinegar, while steaming, on medium fire till it sets. Then cool it over a pan of iced water. Then unmould it on a dish, when it becomes quite cold.

SINGAPORE SOUFFLE   serves 6

4-5 eggs
$1/2$ cup sugar
4 drops of lemon essence
4 or 5 tsps jam or jelly
2 pineapple slices
4 tsps gelatine
4 lemons juice
1 cup cream
$1/4$ tsp red colour

Soak gelatine in 3 tsps of water. Beat eggs and sugar over a pan of water on very slow fire till frothy. Add lemon juice gradually. Dissolve soaked gelatine in one tbsp of boiling water. Add it into beaten eggs and beat it. Add lemon essence and mix it. Pour into round dish and chill. Decorate pineapple slice with cream and jam and again chill. Serve at lunch or dinner.

ICE CREAM

ALMOND CARAMEL ICE CREAM

$1\frac{1}{4}$ cups sugar	5 tsps flour
3 egg yolks	$4\frac{1}{2}$ cups milk
$1\frac{1}{2}$ cups cream	$\frac{1}{2}$ cup sugar for almonds
$\frac{1}{3}$ cup almonds	

Put sugar and unpeeled almonds in frying pan and stir till light brown. Cool and then crush it with rolling pin.

Mix sugar, flour, yolk of eggs with $\frac{1}{2}$ cup of milk. Boil the milk, then in it stir egg mixture till a little thick. Remove from the fire and stir it on a pan of water till cold. Chill and beat it. Now mix lightly whipped cream and crushed almonds. Beat whites of egg till stiff. Mix it into the egg mixture. Line ice cream tin with wax paper and pour the mixture in it. Keep it in freezing chamber till set.

BANANA ICE CREAM   *serves 10*

6 tsps flour	$2\frac{1}{2}$ cups milk
$1\frac{1}{2}$ cups cream	$\frac{1}{3}$ tsp banana essence
2 drops of green colour	2 eggs
$\frac{3}{4}$ cup sugar	

Beat yolk of eggs, milk, sugar and flour together with an egg beater till it becomes smooth. Cook and stir it till it is like custard. Cool and put the mixture in the ice cream tin mould and then keep it in the freezing chamber, till it begins to set. Now remove from the ice cream mould, and beat it with egg beater, beat the white of egg till stiff, then mix it in the ice cream mixture. Whip the chilled cream lightly with egg beater, mix banana essence and green colour into the mixture and then mix cream lightly in it. Line the ice cream mould with wax paper and put the mixture in it, keep it in the freezing chamber and leave it overnight and keep the fridge normal. Remove the ice cream from the mould and cut into slices.

(The milk should be well boiled for 25 minutes, before making the ice cream mixture. Cover the ice cream tin with wax paper and then cover it with lid before setting.)

BANANA ICE CREAM (Italian Style)   serves 6

1 cup mashed ripe banana
$1/2$ cup sugar
$1/4$ tsp salt
1 cup cream
$1/2$ tsp vanilla essence
$1/3$ cup milk
2 tsps lemon juice
2 eggs

Beat egg yolks and sugar till thick and lemon in colour over a pan of hot water. In it mix milk, salt, banana pulp and lemon juice. Cool it. Fold stiff egg whites, essence and thick whipped cream. Put it in freezing trays of refrigerator. Freeze till firm.

LEMON AND VANILLA ICE CREAM (French Style)   serves 8

2 tsps gelatine
$1/2$ tsp vanilla essence
$1/4$ tsp salt
1 cup cream
$1/4$ water
$1\ 1/2$ cups milk
$1/2$ tsp lemon essence
$3/4$ cup sugar
2 eggs

Soak gelatine in water. Beat yolks of egg, milk and sugar and stir over a pan of water on the fire till it coats on the back of a spoon, mix soaked gelatine till dissolved. Cool and mix salt, vanilla and lemon essence and then fold lightly whipped cream. Put it in freezing compartment till $3/4$ set. Then put it in chilled bowl. Mix unbeaten whites of egg and beat it with rotary egg beater till fluffy. Line the ice cream tin with wax paper, pour the mixture in it and again keep it in freezing compartment till firm.

MANGO ICE CREAM
serves 10

1 cup sugar
1 cup mango pulp (chill it)
1½ cups cream
2 eggs
¼ tsp orange colour
3 cups milk (boiled)
6 tsps flour

Mix yolks, sugar and flour into milk and stir it on the fire till it is a little thick. Cool and keep it in freezing chamber till it begins to set and then beat it with egg beater. Beat white of eggs till it becomes stiff, mix into ice cream mixture. Mix colour and mango pulp lightly. Beat chilled cream till a little thick. Mix it in the mixture. Line the ice cream mould with wax paper. Pour the mixture in it, cover with lid and keep it in freezing chamber till set. Cut into slices and serve.

PISTA ICE CREAM
serves 10

1 cup sugar
2 eggs
½ tsp vanilla essence
4 tsps flour
¼ tsp yellow colour
3 cups milk (boiled milk)
⅓ tsp almond essence
1 cup cream
½ cup pistachio
¼ tsp green colour

Mix sugar, flour and yolk of eggs into milk. Stir on fire till a little thick. Cool and keep it in freezing chamber till it begins to set. Beat with egg beater, mix both the essences, colours and peeled and chopped pistachio. Beat the chilled cream till thick. Mix stiff white of egg and cream into egg mixture. Line the ice cream mould with wax paper, in it pour the mixture and cover it with lid. Keep it in freezing chamber and leave it overnight, till set. Cut into slices and serve.

RAINBOW ICE CREAM
serves 12

1 cup sugar
4 eggs
4 tsps cornflour
½ cup water
2 cups cream
2½ cups milk (boiled)

¼ tsp each colour (orange, red, green yellow)

½ tsp cocoa
¼ tsp each essence (orange, strawberry, lemon and pineapple)

Boil sugar and water into a thick syrup, cool it. Beat yolks of egg lightly with one cup of milk and mix into the syrup and cook it over a pan of water till a little thick. Mix cornflour into the rest of the milk and mix it into yolk mixture and stir on fire till thick. Cool it, keep it in freezing chamber till it beings to set. Beat it with egg beater, mix stiff white of egg and then mix chilled and beaten cream. Divide into fine portions, mix colours, essences, and cocoa powder separately. Pour in ice cream mould into alternate layers lined with wax paper and cover with lid and keep in freezing chamber till set and ready to be served.

BISCUITS, PASTRIES AND CAKES

BISCUITS

ALMOND BISCUITS — serves 12

½ cup castor sugar
1 or 1½ eggs
1 tsp lemon essence
25 almonds
1 cup butter
2 cups flour
¾ tsp baking powder

Cream the butter and sugar and in it beat egg. Mix sifted flour, baking powder and coarsely ground unpeeled almonds. Make a slab of dough with hands and chill until firm. Cut about two dozen slices and bake in moderate oven (350° F) until golden brown in colour. Cool, then store in airtight tin. Serve at tea.

ALMOND COOKIES

¾ cup butter
2 cups flour
⅓ cup ground almonds
4 tsps jam
⅛ tsp almond essence
½ cup castor sugar
1 egg
¾ tsp baking powder
a few drops of red colour
¼ tsp lemon

Cream the chilled butter and castor sugar and in it beat egg and essence. Mix sifted flour, baking powder and unpeeled almonds together and in it mix egg mixture lightly on wooden board. Roll it ⅛" thick and cut with fancy cutter. Join both the cookies together with a little beaten egg, bake in moderate oven (350° F) till golden brown. Then cool on a wire rack. Mix colour into the jam and then fill the cavity of cookies with it and serve in paper cases.

CHERRY DREAM COOKIES   serves 8

6 tsps butter $1/_4$ cup castor sugar
$1/_2$ or 1 egg $1/_2$ tsp vanilla essence
1 cup flour   cherry for decoration

Cream chilled butter and sugar together. Add vanilla essence, egg and beat it until fluffy. Add sifted flour and baking powder and mix it lightly. Make 12 round balls of each cookies and press half a cherry into top of each ball. Place on ungreased baking sheets. Bake in moderate oven in (350° F) for 15 or 20 minutes.

CASHEWNUT OR ALMOND BISCUITS   serves 10

$1 1/_4$ cup flour $1/_3$ cup castor sugar
$1/_8$ tsp almond essence $1/_8$ tsp lemon essence
$3/_4$ cup cashewnuts $1/_2$ level tsp baking powder
9 tsps butter $1/_2$ egg

Sift flour, baking powder and castor sugar together, then rub the chilled butter with fingertips. Mix beaten egg, both the essence and mix with fingertips, till the dough is smooth. Roll it $1/_4$ of an inch thick and cut it with a heart-shaped cutter. Mix 2 tsps water with 2 tsps egg (beaten) together. Wet the top of biscuits with it. Crush the cashewnuts to small pieces with rolling pin. Wet the pieces with little water and then sprinkle it on top of biscuits. Put it on ungreased baking tray and bake it in modeate oven (350°) till golden brown. Cool it on wire rack. Serve it at tea or store it in airtight tin.

FANCY BISCUITS   serves 6

1 cup flour   6 tsps butter
1 yolk of egg $1/_4$ cup castor sugar
$1/_2$ tsp baking powder   a little water
$1/_2$ tsp orange essence

Rub the butter into the sifted flour and baking powder with fingertips. Mix yolk of egg and a little water if necessary. Knead into a soft dough. Mix essence, cover and allow to stand on a cool place for 10 minutes. Roll out and cut into shapes with fancy cutters and bake in a moderate oven until light brown in colour. Decorate with chocolate icing.

For Decoration

4 tbsps sifted icing sugar	wax paper for decoration
$1/2$ white of egg	pinch of citric acid
	2 tsps cocoa

Put all the ingredients in a bowl and beat it until it becomes smooth. Decorate the biscuits with this icing.

(If the icing is thick then mix a little white of egg and if it is thin, mix a little icing sugar.)

FANCY CHOCOLATE CREAM BISCUITS

$3/4$ cup butter	$1/2$ cup castor sugar
2 eggs	2 cups flour
$1/4$ tsp vanilla essence	$1/4$ tsp baking powder

Cream the butter and sugar until fluffy, then add eggs and vanilla essence and beat it. Put sifted flour, baking powder on the wooden board and mix the egg mixture lightly. If the dough is too soft, add flour and mix it. Roll it $1/8$" thick and cut it with round cutter. Bake in moderate oven (350° F) until light brown. Cool it, then join the two biscuits together with chocolate butter icing. Decorate with hard chocolate icing.

Chocolate Butter Icing

6 tsps butter	1 tsp cocoa
$1/3$ cup castor sugar	a little water

Cream the butter and sugar until fluffy and in it mix cocoa. If too thick, then add a little water and make it soft. Spread it on the biscuit. Decorate the top of biscuit with it and sprinkle icing sugar. For thick chocolate icing take a little chocolate butter icing and in it mix 1 tsp cocoa and make a thick paste.

LEMON AND ALMOND COOKIES   serves 12

$1 1/2$ cups flour	$1/4$ tsp salt
3 tsp butter	9 cups ghee
1 or 2 eggs	$1/2$ cup sugar

a few drops of lemon
   and almond essence
$1/_4$ cup blanched almonds

Cream the butter, ghee, sugar and in it beat egg and essence. Sift flour and salt together and then mix into cream mixture. Make $2^1/_2$ dozen cookies of fancy shape with rosette tube and put on baking tray lined with brown paper, then decorate ingredients with coarsely ground almonds. Chill it on ice. Bake in moderate oven (350° F) until light brown. Cool and serve at tea.

LEMON PEEL BISCUITS   serves 6 to 8

1 cup (pressed) flour $1/_2$ tsp baking powder
$1/_2$ tsp salt   6 tsps butter
$1/_2$ cup sugar $1/_4$ tsp grated lemon rind
$1/_2$ egg   a few drops of lemon
4 tsps honey   essence
$1/_3$ cup finely chopped peels

Sift flour, baking powder, salt. Cream the butter, and sugar in it, mix egg, essence, honey, lemon rind and beat it. Now mix sifted ingredients. Take a dough in tsp and then make a round ball and put it on greased baking sheet. Flatten or press with fork and decorate with peels. Bake in moderate oven (350°) for about 15 mts. Cool on wire rack and it is ready for serving.

LEMON WAFERS

$1/_2$ cup butter   2 cups flour
$1/_2$ cup castor sugar   1 small egg
$1/_4$ tsp lemon essence $1/_4$ tsp almond
$1/_2$ cup fine chopped   1 tsp baking powder
   lemon peels

Cream the chilled butter, then add egg and beat it. Now mix almond and lemon essence; sift flour, baking powder on a wooden board and then mix egg mixture and mix it lightly. Roll it $1/_4$" thick and cut it with a fancy cutter and brush it with beaten egg and decorate with lemon peels. Bake in moderate oven till golden brown. Remove from the oven and cool. Serve at tea.

BANANA FRITTERS *serves 8*

5 bananas
2 eggs
$1/2$ tsp salt
2 tsps sugar
ghee for frying

1 cup cream
12 tsps flour
1 level tsp baking powder
2 tbsps water

Peel bananas and then cut into long 4 pieces. Beat lightly egg yolks, flour, salt, sugar and water with a wooden spoon. Whisk whites of egg until frothy. Add baking powder into the mixture and fry in hot ghee. Drain on paper, whip cream lightly with 1 tbsp of castor sugar. Serve hot with cream at lunch or dinner. Without cream serve at tea.

DOUGHNUTS *serves 10*

1 heaped cup flour
$1/3$ tsp vanilla essence
$1/4$ tsp soda bi-carbonate
$1/2$ tsp baking powder
1 small egg or $1/2$ big egg

9 tsps sugar (fine)
3 tsps curd (if sour, 2 tsps)
ghee for frying
1 level tsp ghee (unmelted)
$1/3$ cup thick sugar

Sift flour, baking powder and soda bicarbonate. In it mix beaten egg, curd, ghee, vanilla essence and knead till the dough is smooth. Roll it $1/4$" thick and cut it with a doughnut cutter. First fry 4 or 5 doughnuts at a time on medium fire in hot ghee (but not very hot ghee) till they become double in size, then on slow fire till golden brown. Then immediately coat them with thick sugar. Serve at tea.

PASTRIES & CAKES

COFFEE PASTRY *serves 12*

3 eggs
$3/4$ cup flour

$1/2$ cup sugar
1 tsp camp coffee

Beat eggs and sugar in a bowl over a pan of hot water until frothy. Mix sifted flour lightly and mix camp coffee. Pour into greased baking tray and dust with flour. Bake in moderate oven (350° F) until wooden pick comes out smoothly. Cool and cut into one layer and spread butter icing.

Butter Icing
3/4 cup butter
1/2 tsp camp coffee
1/2 cup fondant

Cream the butter and icing sugar and mix essence, spread it on a layer of pastry and keep it in fridge for 15 minutes. Cut pastry into medium sized pieces and then spread a little apricot jam.

Coffee Icing
1 1/2 cups icing sugar
1 tsp butter
3 or 4 tsps water
2 tsps camp coffee

Put all the ingredients in a vessel except camp coffee and then melt on slow fire over a pan of hot water until it becomes into liquid. Mix camp coffee and pour it over the pastry.
(Camp coffee is coffee essence.)

DRY COCONUT PASTRY   *serves 12*

1 cup flour
6 tsps butter
1/2 tsp baking powder
1/2 cup castor sugar
1 egg

Cream the butter and sugar and in it beat egg. Sift flour and baking powder and put on wooden board and mix egg mixture lightly. Roll it 1/8 inch thick and then cut with fancy cutter and line the 18 round pastry moulds with it.

Filling for the Pastry
9 tsps butter
2 eggs
1/2 cup grated dry coconut
1/2 tsp baking powder
1/2 cup sugar
1/2 cup flour
1/2 tsp vanilla essence

Cream the butter and sugar and then beat in yolks and essence until fluffy. Sift flour and baking powder and mix it lightly in egg mixture with coconut. Mix white of egg. Fill in 18 pastry moulds and bake in moderate oven (350° F). Insert wooden pick, if it comes out smoothly then they are done. Cool and then sift icing sugar on it. Serve at tea.

JAM TART   *serves 10*

1 cup flour
4 tsps butter
1 tsp baking powder
4 tsps castor sugar
$1/2$ tsp vanilla essence
1 egg

Sift flour, baking powder and castor sugar and in it rub chilled butter with fingertips. Mix beaten eggs and essence till dough is smooth. Roll it $1/4$" thick. Cut it with fancy round cutter. Then line the pastry mould with it and bake it (350° F) till golden brown. Fill the jam filling.

Filling
$1/4$ tsp red colour
$1/2$ cup apricot or apple jam
1 tsp chopped pistachio

Mix colour in jam and fill it in tart, sprinkle chopped pistachio and then decorate it.

Decoration
2 tsps butter   4 tsps icing sugar

Mix butter and icing sugar together till smooth and decorate the edges with thick butter icing. Put it in paper cases.

STRAWABERRY PASTRY WITH DECORATION   *serves 12*

2 eggs
$1/3$ cup sugar
1 cup cream
$1/4$ tsp strawberry essence for the cream
$1/2$ cup flour
$1/2$ tsp strawberry essence
$1/3$ cup level icing sugar
2 drops of red colour

Beat the eggs and sugar over the pan of water till it becomes frothy. Mix sifted flour lightly and mix $1/2$ tsp strawberry essence. Grease the 18 boat-shaped moulds with ghee and dust with flour. Pour the mixture in them and then bake in moderate oven, till wooden pick comes out smoothly. Cool in airtight tin and then cut into one layer, beat the cream with icing sugar, then mix $1/4$ tsp strawberry essence till it is a little thick. Spread it on the layers and on top of the pastry. Whip the rest of the cream a little thicker than the first time. Add red colour and don't mix it. Now decorate the pastry with cream, put it in pastry paper cases.

SWISS ROLLS   serves 8

$3/4$ cup flour $1/2$ cup sugar
3 eggs   3 or 4 tbsps jam
$1/4$ tsp red colour $1/2$ tsp vanilla essence
$1/2$ cup peeled almonds

Put eggs and sugar in the bowl and beat over a pan of hot water until thick and frothy. Fold sifted flour and essence lightly. Turn into a greased square tin, dust with flour and bake in a moderate oven until tester comes out dry. Cool it, then cut into one layer. Roll it with paper and then spread the jam mixed with red colour, roll up firmly with paper and keep for 10 minutes in a cool place. Then cut into thick slices and put all the slices together; spread a little jam on the sides of rolls and then sprinkle chopped and light brown almonds on it. Put it in pastry paper cases. Serve at tea.

LEMON TART   serves 6

$1/4$ tsp baking powder $1/2$ tsp flour
3 tsps butter $1/2$ small egg
$1/4$ tsp lemon essence   4 tsp castor sugar

Sift flour, baking powder and castor sugar together and in it mix chilled butter with fingertips on the wooden board, lemon essence and $1/2$ egg (beaten). Make a smooth dough. Dust it with flour and roll it $1/4$" thick. Cut it with a round cutter and line it in pastry tins. Bake them in moderate oven (350° F) till golden brown. Cool it and then fill the lemon cheese.

Lemon Cheese
2 yolks of eggs   1 white of egg
6 tsps sugar $1 1/2$ or $1 3/4$ tsps lemon
1 drop of orange colour   juice
3 tsps butter $1/4$ tsp lemon essence
2 drops of yellow colour

Cook all the ingredients together over a pan of hot water on slow fire till it becomes thick and stir it constantly. Then pass it through a sieve. Cool it on the ice or in the fridge till it becomes thick. Decorate the tarts using a big nozzle and put it in paper cases. Serve it.

CHOCOLATE ALMOND STICKS CAKE   serves 6

$3/4$ cup flour   3 tsps cocoa
$1/2$ cup sugar   3 eggs

Sieve flour and cocoa together. Put eggs and sugar in the basin and whisk it over a pan of hot water till thick and frothy. Fold sifted flour and cocoa lightly. Put this mixture in the greased square tin and bake it in moderate oven as soon as possible. Remove from mould, cool on wire rack. Cut into two layers and rejoin it with chocolate cream icing. Cut two thin slices of cake from the cake for cake crumbs.

Chocolate Cream Icing

$1/2$ cup butter $1/3$ cup castor sugar
2 tsps cocoa   3 tsps cold water

Beat the butter, cocoa and water till smooth and creamy. Use this chocolate cream icing on the layers, sides and top of the cake. Coat the sides with cake crumbs.

FANCY COCONUT CAKE   serves 8

$1/2$ cup butter $3/4$ cup sugar
4 eggs $1/4$ tsp red raspberry
$1/2$ cup flour   colour
$1/2$ tsp baking powder $1/2$ tsp vanilla essence
$1/2$ cup grated dry cocoanut

Cream the chilled butter and sugar and in it beat yolks of egg. Mix sifted, baking powder, grated coconut and essence. Mix white of egg lightly. In half of the mixture mix red raspberry colour. Grease the jelly mould and then dust with flour and in it pour the red mixture and then the yellow one and bake it in moderate oven (350° F) until the wooden pick comes out smoothly. Cool it and keep it in airtight tin for 4 hours. Then decorate with sifted icing sugar. Serve at tea.

LEMON AND CHOCOLATE CAKE serves 8

1 cup flour
3/4 cup sugar
4 eggs
1/2 tsp lemon essence
2 tbsps milk

1 tsp baking powder
3/4 cup butter
1 tsp yellow colour
2 tsps cocoa
4 tsps icing sugar

Cream the butter and sugar until frothy and beat egg one by one in it. Mix sifted flour and baking powder lightly. Take 3/4 egg mixture and in it mix lemon essence and yellow colour. To the remaining egg mixture add cocoa and mix it lightly and then mix milk. Grease the jelly mould and in it first pour chocolate mixture and then lemon coloured mixture. Bake in moderate oven (350° F). Insert wooden pick into it, if it comes out smoothly then it is done. Cool in an airtight tin, then decorate with icing sugar.

LEMON LOAF CAKE serves 8

6 eggs
1 cup sugar
1/3 cup lemon peels
2 drops of lemon essence

12 tsps butter
1 3/4 cups flour
1 tsp baking powder
a few drops of yellow colour

Cut lemon peels into long and thin slices. Beat eggs and sugar over the pan of hot water until frothy. Add melted butter gradually and then sifted flour and baking powder, and 2 oz lemon peels and mix it lightly, mix colour and essence. Line the mould with greased brown paper. Put the butter in the mould and sprinkle 1/2 oz lemon peels on the top. Bake in moderate oven for 3/4 or 1 hour. Test it by wooden pick. Cool and put it in an airtight tin. Cut the slices about 1/4 inch thick. Serve at tea.

PLAIN FRUIT CAKE serves 6

3 eggs
3/4 cup flour
3/4 tsp baking powder
1/2 cup raisins, almonds and cherry

9 tsps butter
1/2 cup sugar
1/2 tsp vanilla essence

Cream the butter and sugar and then in it beat eggs one by one until fluffy. Add sifted flour and baking powder and mix it lightly. Mix vanilla essence and fruit. Line the tin with greased brown paper. Pour the mixture in it. Bake in moderate oven (350° F). Thrust wooden pick in it, if it comes out smoothly, then it is done; remove from oven. Cool it on wire rack and keep it in airtight tin for four hours. Serve at tea. (Wash the fruit and then dry with clean cloth. Do not serve cake while hot.)

PLUM CAKE serves 8

3/4 cup butter
1 cup flour
2 tsps caramel syrup
1/2 level tsp ground cinnamon
1/2 cup sugar
4 eggs
1/4 tsp grated nutmeg
2 cups fruit (cherry, lemon, orange, peels, petha raisins and almonds)

Line the tin with greased brown paper. Cream the butter and sugar, then in it beat eggs one by one. Add caramel syrup, grated nutmeg, ground cinnamon and mix it. Fold the flour lightly into egg mixture. Mix chopped fruit. Pour the mixture in lined square tin and bake it in moderate oven (350° F) until a wooden pick thrust into cake comes out clean. Immediately remove from oven, cool and put it in airtight tin. Serve at tea. This cake can be kept for 4 weeks.

QUEEN'S CAKE serves 6

1/3 cup butter
3 eggs
1/2 tsp lemon essence
3/4 cup flour
1/2 cup sugar
1/4 tsp almond essence
1/2 tsp baking powder
1/2 cup blanched and ground almonds

Cream the butter and sugar, then add yolks of egg and beat it until fluffy. Sift baking powder and flour together and mix it into yolk mixture with ground almond and lemon essence. Mix white of the eggs. Pour in greased loaf tin and sprinkle 1/4 oz almonds on the top of batter and bake in moderate oven (350° F). Thrust wooden pick in it, if it comes out smoothly then it is ready. Cool and keep it in airtight tin for four hours and then serve.

SMALL FANCY CAKES serves 12

9 tsps butter
3 eggs
1/4 cup dry grated coconut
cherries and 2 tbsps dry grated coconut for decoration
3/4 cup sugar
1/2 tsp baking powder
3/4 cup) flour
3 tsps icing sugar

Cream the butter and sugar, then beat in yolks. Mix sifted flour, baking powder, essence and coconut. Mix white of eggs lightly into yolk mixture. Line the small pastry tins with paper cases, then pour the mixture $3/4$ full and then sprinkle grated coconut and bake in moderate oven (350° F) till wooden pick comes out smoothly. Cool on wire rack and keep it in airtight tin for 4 hours. Stick cherry with jam on each cake and then sift icing sugar. Serve at tea.

SPICED FRUIT CAKE serves 8

2 cups flour
1/4 tsp soda bicarbonate
1/2 tsp ground cinnamon
1/4 level tsp ground clove
1/2 cup blanched and sliced almonds
2 cups glazed peels and cherry
1 tsp baking powder
1/2 level tsp ground nutmeg
3 eggs
1 cup raisins
1/2 level tsp salt
1/2 cup honey
1 cup heaped brown sugar
3/4 cup butter

Beat butter and brown sugar till fluffy and in it beat eggs. Mix sifted flour, baking powder, soda bicorbonate, salt and spices together. Then mix honey and fruit, dusted with flour. Line the loaf tin with greased brown paper and in it pour the cake mixture. Bake it (in 350° F) till wooden pick comes out smoothly. Cool it on wire rack and peel off paper and then store in a tightly closed cake box.

STRAWBERRY CAKE WITH DECORATION

serves 6

4 eggs
$3/4$ cup sugar
1 cup flour
$1/4$ tsp strawberry essence

Beat the eggs and sugar over a pan of hot water till it becomes frothy. Mix sifted flour and strawberry essence. Grease the big round mould with ghee and then dust with flour. Pour the mixture in it and bake in moderate oven till the wooden pick comes out smoothly. Cool on the wire rack. Put it in the same mould covered with cloth for 6 hours. Cut into three layers and cut a very thin layer from the top for cake crumbs. Then spread butter icing.

Butter Icing

$3/4$ cup butter
$1/4$ cup of water
$1/3$ cup icing sugar
$1/4$ cup of water
$1/4$ tsp strawberry essence

Beat all the ingredients together except water with wooden spoon till it becomes creamy. Mix water (iced cold water in summer and lukewarm in winter). Spread it on the layers of the cake. Keep the leftover butter icing for the sides.

Then spread any smooth jam on the top of cake and spread glaze icing.

Glaze Icing

$1 1/2$ cup icing sugar
$1/8$ tsp strawberry essence
$1/8$ drop of red colour
4 or 5 tsps water
1 level tsp butter

Put all the ingredients together in a small bowl and cook it over a pan of hot water till it becomes liquid. Pour it immediately over the cake. Spread with butter icing on the sides and coat it with cake crumbs. Decorate with royal icing.

Royal Icing

$3/4$ or 1 cup of icing sugar
1 or 2 drops of red colour
1 white of egg
1 or 2 drops of green colour

Beat the icing sugar and white of egg (little by little) together and beat it till it becomes white in colour and stands errect with spoon. Cover with a wet cloth. Divide into four portions. Three portions keep in white and in fourth portion (divide into two) mix red and green colour separately. Decorate the cake with it.

WHITE FRUIT CAKE   serves 12

2 cups flour
1 tsp raspberry essence
$1\frac{1}{2}$ tsps baking powder
12 tsps butter
1 cup
4 egg whites
$1\frac{1}{2}$ cups castor sugar
$\frac{1}{2}$ cup milk
1 tsp salt
preserved greeen and red coloured pumpkin

Grease the pastry moulds and then dust with flour. Sift flour, sugar, baking powder and salt and put in the bowl. Add melted butter, milk, raspberry essence and beat for two minutes. Mix egg whites and beat and for a few minutes. Fold the chopped coloured pumpkin in the mixture. Pour into moulds. Bake in moderate oven (350° F) for 35 minutes. Insert wooden pick into cake, if it comes out smoothly then it is ready. Cool and put in an airtight tin. Serve at tea.

MANGO BREAD   serves 10

3 or $3\frac{1}{4}$ cups flour
$1\frac{3}{4}$ cups sugar
$1\frac{1}{2}$ tsps baking powder
$\frac{1}{2}$ cup melted butter
2 big eggs (3 or 4 small)
1 cup mango pulp
$\frac{1}{2}$ tsp soda bicarbonate

Beat eggs and sugar with wooden spoon. Then in it mix melted butter and mango pulp. Mix sifted flour, baking powder, soda bicarbonate. Grease the loaf tin with ghee and dust with flour. Pour the mixture in it and bake in moderate oven till wooden pick comes out smoothly. Cool on the wire rack, then keep it covered with cloth in an airtight box.

WALNUT DECORATED CAKE *serves 8*

3 or 4 eggs 1 cup flour
$^3/_4$ cup sugar $^1/_2$ tsp vanilla essence

Put eggs and sugar in a bowl and beat over a pan of hot water until stiff and frothy. Mix sifted flour lightly and then mix vanilla essence. Pour into greased square tin and bake in a moderate oven (350° F) for 25 minutes. Prick a thin wooden pick, if it comes out smoothly then it is ready. Cool the cake and cut into two layers.

Butter Icing

$^3/_4$ cup butter $^1/_3$ cup icing sugar
1 cup walnuts $^1/_2$ tsp vanilla essence
a few drops of yellow colour

Cream the butter, icing sugar and vanilla essence and then mix yellow colour. Spread half the butter on the layers and keep the rest for the sides. Grind coarsely walnuts. Sprinkle syrup on the top cake (3 tsps sugar and 4 tsps water). Put in vessel and cook until sticky.

Glaze Icing

1 heaped cup icing sugar a few drops of yellow colour
2 or 3 tsps water 1 tsp butter

Put all ingredients in a bowl on a slow fire and stir until it becomes a thick liquid. Remove from fire, add yellow colour and mix well. Pour over the cake and then keep for 10 minutes to set. Spread the butter icing on the sides of cake and coat with walnuts.

Royal Icing

$1^1/_4$ cup icing sugar 1 white of egg
pinch of citric acid 4 pieces of cherry
a few drops of red and
    green colour

Beat icing sugar, white of egg and citric acid until smooth. Keep a little icing for the leaves and to the rest add red colour and mix well. Decorate the cake with it and cherry.

Books on COOKERY

COOKERY

Punjabi Cooking
ISBN 81 207 0179 8, Rs. 60

A Cook's Tour of South India
ISBN 81 207 0947 0, Rs. 60

Non-Veg. Indian Cookery
ISBN 81 207 1408 3, Rs. 60

Indian Cooking Overseas
ISBN 81 207 1613 2, Rs. 65

Indian Cook Book
ISBN 81 207 0542 4, Rs. 60

Chinese Cookery
ISBN 81 207 0938 1, Rs. 90

Party Cuisine
ISBN 81 207 1534 9, Rs. 55

Indian Cookery
ISBN 81 207 0018 x, Rs. 50

Delights of Indian Appetizers
ISBN 81 207 1353 2, Rs. 45

Indian & Mughlai Rice Treats
ISBN 81 207 1070 3, Rs. 45

Cooking the Healthy Way
ISBN 81 207 1354 0, Rs. 45

GOURMET'S CHOICE

Cakes
ISBN 81 207 1749 x, Rs. 35

Salads
ISBN 81 207 1750 3, Rs. 35

Seafood
ISBN 81 207 1751 1, Rs. 35

Soups
ISBN 81 207 1752 x, Rs. 35

Potato Delights
ISBN 81 207 1734 1, Rs. 30

Soups
ISBN 81 207 1732 5, Rs. 30

Meat Delights
ISBN 81 207 1741 4, Rs. 30

Chocolate Delights
ISBN 81 207 1736 8, Rs. 30

Chinese Cuisine
ISBN 81 207 1733 3, Rs. 30

Desserts
ISBN 81 207 1739 2, Rs. 30

Pasta Delights
ISBN 81 207 1738 4, Rs. 30

Barbecue
ISBN 81 207 1735 x, Rs. 30

COOKING IS FUN

Cakes
ISBN 81 207 1693 0, Rs. 30

Cocktails
ISBN 81 207 1694 9, Rs. 30

Mughlai
ISBN 81 207 1692 2, Rs. 30

Salads
ISBN 81 207 1695 7, Rs. 30

Egg Delights
ISBN 81 207 1786 4, Rs. 30

Vegetable Delights
ISBN 81 207 1730 9, Rs. 30

Breakfast Delights
ISBN 81 207 1789 9, Rs. 30

Seafood
ISBN 81 207 1854 2, Rs. 30